CS-10   GENERAL APTITUDE AND ABILITIES SERIES

This is your
PASSBOOK for...

Vocabulary/ Word Meaning

Test Preparation Study Guide
Questions & Answers

COPYRIGHT NOTICE

This book is SOLELY intended for, is sold ONLY to, and its use is RESTRICTED to individual, bona fide applicants or candidates who qualify by virtue of having seriously filed applications for appropriate license, certificate, professional and/or promotional advancement, higher school matriculation, scholarship, or other legitimate requirements of education and/or governmental authorities.

This book is NOT intended for use, class instruction, tutoring, training, duplication, copying, reprinting, excerption, or adaptation, etc., by:

1) Other publishers
2) Proprietors and/or Instructors of "Coaching" and/or Preparatory Courses
3) Personnel and/or Training Divisions of commercial, industrial, and governmental organizations
4) Schools, colleges, or universities and/or their departments and staffs, including teachers and other personnel
5) Testing Agencies or Bureaus
6) Study groups which seek by the purchase of a single volume to copy and/or duplicate and/or adapt this material for use by the group as a whole without having purchased individual volumes for each of the members of the group
7) Et al.

Such persons would be in violation of appropriate Federal and State statutes.

PROVISION OF LICENSING AGREEMENTS – Recognized educational, commercial, industrial, and governmental institutions and organizations, and others legitimately engaged in educational pursuits, including training, testing, and measurement activities, may address request for a licensing agreement to the copyright owners, who will determine whether, and under what conditions, including fees and charges, the materials in this book may be used them. In other words, a licensing facility exists for the legitimate use of the material in this book on other than an individual basis. However, it is asseverated and affirmed here that the material in this book CANNOT be used without the receipt of the express permission of such a licensing agreement from the Publishers. Inquiries re licensing should be addressed to the company, attention rights and permissions department.

All rights reserved, including the right of reproduction in whole or in part, in any form or by any means, electronic or mechanical, including photocopying, recording, or by any information storage and retrieval system, without permission in writing from the Publisher.

Copyright © 2024 by
National Learning Corporation

212 Michael Drive, Syosset, NY 11791
(516) 921-8888 • www.passbooks.com
E-mail: info@passbooks.com

PUBLISHED IN THE UNITED STATES OF AMERICA

PASSBOOK® SERIES

THE *PASSBOOK® SERIES* has been created to prepare applicants and candidates for the ultimate academic battlefield – the examination room.

At some time in our lives, each and every one of us may be required to take an examination – for validation, matriculation, admission, qualification, registration, certification, or licensure.

Based on the assumption that every applicant or candidate has met the basic formal educational standards, has taken the required number of courses, and read the necessary texts, the *PASSBOOK® SERIES* furnishes the one special preparation which may assure passing with confidence, instead of failing with insecurity. Examination questions – together with answers – are furnished as the basic vehicle for study so that the mysteries of the examination and its compounding difficulties may be eliminated or diminished by a sure method.

This book is meant to help you pass your examination provided that you qualify and are serious in your objective.

The entire field is reviewed through the huge store of content information which is succinctly presented through a provocative and challenging approach – the question-and-answer method.

A climate of success is established by furnishing the correct answers at the end of each test.

You soon learn to recognize types of questions, forms of questions, and patterns of questioning. You may even begin to anticipate expected outcomes.

You perceive that many questions are repeated or adapted so that you can gain acute insights, which may enable you to score many sure points.

You learn how to confront new questions, or types of questions, and to attack them confidently and work out the correct answers.

You note objectives and emphases, and recognize pitfalls and dangers, so that you may make positive educational adjustments.

Moreover, you are kept fully informed in relation to new concepts, methods, practices, and directions in the field.

You discover that you are actually taking the examination all the time: you are preparing for the examination by "taking" an examination, not by reading extraneous and/or supererogatory textbooks.

In short, this PASSBOOK®, used directedly, should be an important factor in helping you to pass your test.

CIVIL SERVICE VOCABULARY / WORD MEANING

The General Aptitude and Abilities Series provides functional, intensive test practice and drill in the basic skills and areas common to many civil service, general aptitude and achievement examinations necessary for entrance into schools or occupations.

Passbooks in this series use a variety of question types, and other applicable items like charts, graphs, illustrations and more, to prepare candidates for testing in particular subject areas. This Passbook features a wide range of questions covering vocabulary and word meaning.

HOW TO TAKE A TEST

I. YOU MUST PASS AN EXAMINATION

A. *WHAT EVERY CANDIDATE SHOULD KNOW*

Examination applicants often ask us for help in preparing for the written test. What can I study in advance? What kinds of questions will be asked? How will the test be given? How will the papers be graded?

As an applicant for a civil service examination, you may be wondering about some of these things. Our purpose here is to suggest effective methods of advance study and to describe civil service examinations.

Your chances for success on this examination can be increased if you know how to prepare. Those "pre-examination jitters" can be reduced if you know what to expect. You can even experience an adventure in good citizenship if you know why civil service exams are given.

B. *WHY ARE CIVIL SERVICE EXAMINATIONS GIVEN?*

Civil service examinations are important to you in two ways. As a citizen, you want public jobs filled by employees who know how to do their work. As a job seeker, you want a fair chance to compete for that job on an equal footing with other candidates. The best-known means of accomplishing this two-fold goal is the competitive examination.

Exams are widely publicized throughout the nation. They may be administered for jobs in federal, state, city, municipal, town or village governments or agencies.

Any citizen may apply, with some limitations, such as the age or residence of applicants. Your experience and education may be reviewed to see whether you meet the requirements for the particular examination. When these requirements exist, they are reasonable and applied consistently to all applicants. Thus, a competitive examination may cause you some uneasiness now, but it is your privilege and safeguard.

C. *HOW ARE CIVIL SERVICE EXAMS DEVELOPED?*

Examinations are carefully written by trained technicians who are specialists in the field known as "psychological measurement," in consultation with recognized authorities in the field of work that the test will cover. These experts recommend the subject matter areas or skills to be tested; only those knowledges or skills important to your success on the job are included. The most reliable books and source materials available are used as references. Together, the experts and technicians judge the difficulty level of the questions.

Test technicians know how to phrase questions so that the problem is clearly stated. Their ethics do not permit "trick" or "catch" questions. Questions may have been tried out on sample groups, or subjected to statistical analysis, to determine their usefulness.

Written tests are often used in combination with performance tests, ratings of training and experience, and oral interviews. All of these measures combine to form the best-known means of finding the right person for the right job.

II. HOW TO PASS THE WRITTEN TEST

A. NATURE OF THE EXAMINATION

To prepare intelligently for civil service examinations, you should know how they differ from school examinations you have taken. In school you were assigned certain definite pages to read or subjects to cover. The examination questions were quite detailed and usually emphasized memory. Civil service exams, on the other hand, try to discover your present ability to perform the duties of a position, plus your potentiality to learn these duties. In other words, a civil service exam attempts to predict how successful you will be. Questions cover such a broad area that they cannot be as minute and detailed as school exam questions.

In the public service similar kinds of work, or positions, are grouped together in one "class." This process is known as *position-classification*. All the positions in a class are paid according to the salary range for that class. One class title covers all of these positions, and they are all tested by the same examination.

B. FOUR BASIC STEPS

1) Study the announcement

How, then, can you know what subjects to study? Our best answer is: "Learn as much as possible about the class of positions for which you've applied." The exam will test the knowledge, skills and abilities needed to do the work.

Your most valuable source of information about the position you want is the official exam announcement. This announcement lists the training and experience qualifications. Check these standards and apply only if you come reasonably close to meeting them.

The brief description of the position in the examination announcement offers some clues to the subjects which will be tested. Think about the job itself. Review the duties in your mind. Can you perform them, or are there some in which you are rusty? Fill in the blank spots in your preparation.

Many jurisdictions preview the written test in the exam announcement by including a section called "Knowledge and Abilities Required," "Scope of the Examination," or some similar heading. Here you will find out specifically what fields will be tested.

2) Review your own background

Once you learn in general what the position is all about, and what you need to know to do the work, ask yourself which subjects you already know fairly well and which need improvement. You may wonder whether to concentrate on improving your strong areas or on building some background in your fields of weakness. When the announcement has specified "some knowledge" or "considerable knowledge," or has used adjectives like "beginning principles of..." or "advanced ... methods," you can get a clue as to the number and difficulty of questions to be asked in any given field. More questions, and hence broader coverage, would be included for those subjects which are more important in the work. Now weigh your strengths and weaknesses against the job requirements and prepare accordingly.

3) Determine the level of the position

Another way to tell how intensively you should prepare is to understand the level of the job for which you are applying. Is it the entering level? In other words, is this the position in which beginners in a field of work are hired? Or is it an intermediate or advanced level? Sometimes this is indicated by such words as "Junior" or "Senior" in the class title. Other jurisdictions use Roman numerals to designate the level – Clerk I, Clerk II, for example. The word "Supervisor" sometimes appears in the title. If the level is not indicated by the title, check the description of duties. Will you be working under very close supervision, or will you have responsibility for independent decisions in this work?

4) Choose appropriate study materials

Now that you know the subjects to be examined and the relative amount of each subject to be covered, you can choose suitable study materials. For beginning level jobs, or even advanced ones, if you have a pronounced weakness in some aspect of your training, read a modern, standard textbook in that field. Be sure it is up to date and has general coverage. Such books are normally available at your library, and the librarian will be glad to help you locate one. For entry-level positions, questions of appropriate difficulty are chosen -- neither highly advanced questions, nor those too simple. Such questions require careful thought but not advanced training.

If the position for which you are applying is technical or advanced, you will read more advanced, specialized material. If you are already familiar with the basic principles of your field, elementary textbooks would waste your time. Concentrate on advanced textbooks and technical periodicals. Think through the concepts and review difficult problems in your field.

These are all general sources. You can get more ideas on your own initiative, following these leads. For example, training manuals and publications of the government agency which employs workers in your field can be useful, particularly for technical and professional positions. A letter or visit to the government department involved may result in more specific study suggestions, and certainly will provide you with a more definite idea of the exact nature of the position you are seeking.

III. KINDS OF TESTS

Tests are used for purposes other than measuring knowledge and ability to perform specified duties. For some positions, it is equally important to test ability to make adjustments to new situations or to profit from training. In others, basic mental abilities not dependent on information are essential. Questions which test these things may not appear as pertinent to the duties of the position as those which test for knowledge and information. Yet they are often highly important parts of a fair examination. For very general questions, it is almost impossible to help you direct your study efforts. What we can do is to point out some of the more common of these general abilities needed in public service positions and describe some typical questions.

1) General information

Broad, general information has been found useful for predicting job success in some kinds of work. This is tested in a variety of ways, from vocabulary lists to questions about current events. Basic background in some field of work, such as sociology or economics, may be sampled in a group of questions. Often these are principles which have become familiar to most persons through exposure rather than through formal training. It is difficult to advise you how to study for these questions; being alert to the world around you is our best suggestion.

2) Verbal ability

An example of an ability needed in many positions is verbal or language ability. Verbal ability is, in brief, the ability to use and understand words. Vocabulary and grammar tests are typical measures of this ability. Reading comprehension or paragraph interpretation questions are common in many kinds of civil service tests. You are given a paragraph of written material and asked to find its central meaning.

3) Numerical ability

Number skills can be tested by the familiar arithmetic problem, by checking paired lists of numbers to see which are alike and which are different, or by interpreting charts and graphs. In the latter test, a graph may be printed in the test booklet which you are asked to use as the basis for answering questions.

4) Observation

A popular test for law-enforcement positions is the observation test. A picture is shown to you for several minutes, then taken away. Questions about the picture test your ability to observe both details and larger elements.

5) Following directions

In many positions in the public service, the employee must be able to carry out written instructions dependably and accurately. You may be given a chart with several columns, each column listing a variety of information. The questions require you to carry out directions involving the information given in the chart.

6) Skills and aptitudes

Performance tests effectively measure some manual skills and aptitudes. When the skill is one in which you are trained, such as typing or shorthand, you can practice. These tests are often very much like those given in business school or high school courses. For many of the other skills and aptitudes, however, no short-time preparation can be made. Skills and abilities natural to you or that you have developed throughout your lifetime are being tested.

Many of the general questions just described provide all the data needed to answer the questions and ask you to use your reasoning ability to find the answers. Your best preparation for these tests, as well as for tests of facts and ideas, is to be at your physical and mental best. You, no doubt, have your own methods of getting into an exam-taking mood and keeping "in shape." The next section lists some ideas on this subject.

IV. KINDS OF QUESTIONS

Only rarely is the "essay" question, which you answer in narrative form, used in civil service tests. Civil service tests are usually of the short-answer type. Full instructions for answering these questions will be given to you at the examination. But in case this is your first experience with short-answer questions and separate answer sheets, here is what you need to know:

1) **Multiple-choice Questions**

Most popular of the short-answer questions is the "multiple choice" or "best answer" question. It can be used, for example, to test for factual knowledge, ability to solve problems or judgment in meeting situations found at work.

A multiple-choice question is normally one of three types—
- It can begin with an incomplete statement followed by several possible endings. You are to find the one ending which *best* completes the statement, although some of the others may not be entirely wrong.
- It can also be a complete statement in the form of a question which is answered by choosing one of the statements listed.

- It can be in the form of a problem – again you select the best answer.

Here is an example of a multiple-choice question with a discussion which should give you some clues as to the method for choosing the right answer:

When an employee has a complaint about his assignment, the action which will *best* help him overcome his difficulty is to
- A. discuss his difficulty with his coworkers
- B. take the problem to the head of the organization
- C. take the problem to the person who gave him the assignment
- D. say nothing to anyone about his complaint

In answering this question, you should study each of the choices to find which is best. Consider choice "A" – Certainly an employee may discuss his complaint with fellow employees, but no change or improvement can result, and the complaint remains unresolved. Choice "B" is a poor choice since the head of the organization probably does not know what assignment you have been given, and taking your problem to him is known as "going over the head" of the supervisor. The supervisor, or person who made the assignment, is the person who can clarify it or correct any injustice. Choice "C" is, therefore, correct. To say nothing, as in choice "D," is unwise. Supervisors have and interest in knowing the problems employees are facing, and the employee is seeking a solution to his problem.

2) True/False Questions

The "true/false" or "right/wrong" form of question is sometimes used. Here a complete statement is given. Your job is to decide whether the statement is right or wrong.

SAMPLE: A roaming cell-phone call to a nearby city costs less than a non-roaming call to a distant city.

This statement is wrong, or false, since roaming calls are more expensive.

This is not a complete list of all possible question forms, although most of the others are variations of these common types. You will always get complete directions for answering questions. Be sure you understand *how* to mark your answers – ask questions until you do.

V. RECORDING YOUR ANSWERS

Computer terminals are used more and more today for many different kinds of exams.

For an examination with very few applicants, you may be told to record your answers in the test booklet itself. Separate answer sheets are much more common. If this separate answer sheet is to be scored by machine – and this is often the case – it is highly important that you mark your answers correctly in order to get credit.

An electronic scoring machine is often used in civil service offices because of the speed with which papers can be scored. Machine-scored answer sheets must be marked with a pencil, which will be given to you. This pencil has a high graphite content which responds to the electronic scoring machine. As a matter of fact, stray dots may register as answers, so do not let your pencil rest on the answer sheet while you are pondering the correct answer. Also, if your pencil lead breaks or is otherwise defective, ask for another.

Since the answer sheet will be dropped in a slot in the scoring machine, be careful not to bend the corners or get the paper crumpled.

The answer sheet normally has five vertical columns of numbers, with 30 numbers to a column. These numbers correspond to the question numbers in your test booklet. After each number, going across the page are four or five pairs of dotted lines. These short dotted lines have small letters or numbers above them. The first two pairs may also have a "T" or "F" above the letters. This indicates that the first two pairs only are to be used if the questions are of the true-false type. If the questions are multiple choice, disregard the "T" and "F" and pay attention only to the small letters or numbers.

Answer your questions in the manner of the sample that follows:

32. The largest city in the United States is
    A. Washington, D.C.
    B. New York City
    C. Chicago
    D. Detroit
    E. San Francisco

1) Choose the answer you think is best. (New York City is the largest, so "B" is correct.)
2) Find the row of dotted lines numbered the same as the question you are answering. (Find row number 32)
3) Find the pair of dotted lines corresponding to the answer. (Find the pair of lines under the mark "B.")
4) Make a solid black mark between the dotted lines.

VI. BEFORE THE TEST

Common sense will help you find procedures to follow to get ready for an examination. Too many of us, however, overlook these sensible measures. Indeed, nervousness and fatigue have been found to be the most serious reasons why applicants fail to do their best on civil service tests. Here is a list of reminders:

- Begin your preparation early – Don't wait until the last minute to go scurrying around for books and materials or to find out what the position is all about.
- Prepare continuously – An hour a night for a week is better than an all-night cram session. This has been definitely established. What is more, a night a week for a month will return better dividends than crowding your study into a shorter period of time.
- Locate the place of the exam – You have been sent a notice telling you when and where to report for the examination. If the location is in a different town or otherwise unfamiliar to you, it would be well to inquire the best route and learn something about the building.
- Relax the night before the test – Allow your mind to rest. Do not study at all that night. Plan some mild recreation or diversion; then go to bed early and get a good night's sleep.
- Get up early enough to make a leisurely trip to the place for the test – This way unforeseen events, traffic snarls, unfamiliar buildings, etc. will not upset you.
- Dress comfortably – A written test is not a fashion show. You will be known by number and not by name, so wear something comfortable.

- Leave excess paraphernalia at home – Shopping bags and odd bundles will get in your way. You need bring only the items mentioned in the official notice you received; usually everything you need is provided. Do not bring reference books to the exam. They will only confuse those last minutes and be taken away from you when in the test room.
- Arrive somewhat ahead of time – If because of transportation schedules you must get there very early, bring a newspaper or magazine to take your mind off yourself while waiting.
- Locate the examination room – When you have found the proper room, you will be directed to the seat or part of the room where you will sit. Sometimes you are given a sheet of instructions to read while you are waiting. Do not fill out any forms until you are told to do so; just read them and be prepared.
- Relax and prepare to listen to the instructions
- If you have any physical problem that may keep you from doing your best, be sure to tell the test administrator. If you are sick or in poor health, you really cannot do your best on the exam. You can come back and take the test some other time.

VII. AT THE TEST

The day of the test is here and you have the test booklet in your hand. The temptation to get going is very strong. Caution! There is more to success than knowing the right answers. You must know how to identify your papers and understand variations in the type of short-answer question used in this particular examination. Follow these suggestions for maximum results from your efforts:

1) Cooperate with the monitor

The test administrator has a duty to create a situation in which you can be as much at ease as possible. He will give instructions, tell you when to begin, check to see that you are marking your answer sheet correctly, and so on. He is not there to guard you, although he will see that your competitors do not take unfair advantage. He wants to help you do your best.

2) Listen to all instructions

Don't jump the gun! Wait until you understand all directions. In most civil service tests you get more time than you need to answer the questions. So don't be in a hurry. Read each word of instructions until you clearly understand the meaning. Study the examples, listen to all announcements and follow directions. Ask questions if you do not understand what to do.

3) Identify your papers

Civil service exams are usually identified by number only. You will be assigned a number; you must not put your name on your test papers. Be sure to copy your number correctly. Since more than one exam may be given, copy your exact examination title.

4) Plan your time

Unless you are told that a test is a "speed" or "rate of work" test, speed itself is usually not important. Time enough to answer all the questions will be provided, but this does not mean that you have all day. An overall time limit has been set. Divide the total time (in minutes) by the number of questions to determine the approximate time you have for each question.

5) Do not linger over difficult questions

If you come across a difficult question, mark it with a paper clip (useful to have along) and come back to it when you have been through the booklet. One caution if you do this – be sure to skip a number on your answer sheet as well. Check often to be sure that you have not lost your place and that you are marking in the row numbered the same as the question you are answering.

6) Read the questions

Be sure you know what the question asks! Many capable people are unsuccessful because they failed to *read* the questions correctly.

7) Answer all questions

Unless you have been instructed that a penalty will be deducted for incorrect answers, it is better to guess than to omit a question.

8) Speed tests

It is often better NOT to guess on speed tests. It has been found that on timed tests people are tempted to spend the last few seconds before time is called in marking answers at random – without even reading them – in the hope of picking up a few extra points. To discourage this practice, the instructions may warn you that your score will be "corrected" for guessing. That is, a penalty will be applied. The incorrect answers will be deducted from the correct ones, or some other penalty formula will be used.

9) Review your answers

If you finish before time is called, go back to the questions you guessed or omitted to give them further thought. Review other answers if you have time.

10) Return your test materials

If you are ready to leave before others have finished or time is called, take ALL your materials to the monitor and leave quietly. Never take any test material with you. The monitor can discover whose papers are not complete, and taking a test booklet may be grounds for disqualification.

VIII. EXAMINATION TECHNIQUES

1) Read the general instructions carefully. These are usually printed on the first page of the exam booklet. As a rule, these instructions refer to the timing of the examination; the fact that you should not start work until the signal and must stop work at a signal, etc. If there are any *special* instructions, such as a choice of questions to be answered, make sure that you note this instruction carefully.

2) When you are ready to start work on the examination, that is as soon as the signal has been given, read the instructions to each question booklet, underline any key words or phrases, such as *least, best, outline, describe* and the like. In this way you will tend to answer as requested rather than discover on reviewing your paper that you *listed without describing*, that you selected the *worst* choice rather than the *best* choice, etc.

3) If the examination is of the objective or multiple-choice type – that is, each question will also give a series of possible answers: A, B, C or D, and you are called upon to select the best answer and write the letter next to that answer on your answer paper – it is advisable to start answering each question in turn. There may be anywhere from 50 to 100 such questions in the three or four hours allotted and you can see how much time would be taken if you read through all the questions before beginning to answer any. Furthermore, if you come across a question or group of questions which you know would be difficult to answer, it would undoubtedly affect your handling of all the other questions.

4) If the examination is of the essay type and contains but a few questions, it is a moot point as to whether you should read all the questions before starting to answer any one. Of course, if you are given a choice – say five out of seven and the like – then it is essential to read all the questions so you can eliminate the two that are most difficult. If, however, you are asked to answer all the questions, there may be danger in trying to answer the easiest one first because you may find that you will spend too much time on it. The best technique is to answer the first question, then proceed to the second, etc.

5) Time your answers. Before the exam begins, write down the time it started, then add the time allowed for the examination and write down the time it must be completed, then divide the time available somewhat as follows:
   - If 3-1/2 hours are allowed, that would be 210 minutes. If you have 80 objective-type questions, that would be an average of 2-1/2 minutes per question. Allow yourself no more than 2 minutes per question, or a total of 160 minutes, which will permit about 50 minutes to review.
   - If for the time allotment of 210 minutes there are 7 essay questions to answer, that would average about 30 minutes a question. Give yourself only 25 minutes per question so that you have about 35 minutes to review.

6) The most important instruction is to *read each question* and make sure you know what is wanted. The second most important instruction is to *time yourself properly* so that you answer every question. The third most important instruction is to *answer every question*. Guess if you have to but include something for each question. Remember that you will receive no credit for a blank and will probably receive some credit if you write something in answer to an essay question. If you guess a letter – say "B" for a multiple-choice question – you may have guessed right. If you leave a blank as an answer to a multiple-choice question, the examiners may respect your feelings but it will not add a point to your score. Some exams may penalize you for wrong answers, so in such cases *only*, you may not want to guess unless you have some basis for your answer.

7) Suggestions
   a. Objective-type questions
      1. Examine the question booklet for proper sequence of pages and questions
      2. Read all instructions carefully
      3. Skip any question which seems too difficult; return to it after all other questions have been answered
      4. Apportion your time properly; do not spend too much time on any single question or group of questions

5. Note and underline key words – *all, most, fewest, least, best, worst, same, opposite*, etc.
6. Pay particular attention to negatives
7. Note unusual option, e.g., unduly long, short, complex, different or similar in content to the body of the question
8. Observe the use of "hedging" words – *probably, may, most likely*, etc.
9. Make sure that your answer is put next to the same number as the question
10. Do not second-guess unless you have good reason to believe the second answer is definitely more correct
11. Cross out original answer if you decide another answer is more accurate; do not erase until you are ready to hand your paper in
12. Answer all questions; guess unless instructed otherwise
13. Leave time for review

b. Essay questions
1. Read each question carefully
2. Determine exactly what is wanted. Underline key words or phrases.
3. Decide on outline or paragraph answer
4. Include many different points and elements unless asked to develop any one or two points or elements
5. Show impartiality by giving pros and cons unless directed to select one side only
6. Make and write down any assumptions you find necessary to answer the questions
7. Watch your English, grammar, punctuation and choice of words
8. Time your answers; don't crowd material

8) Answering the essay question

Most essay questions can be answered by framing the specific response around several key words or ideas. Here are a few such key words or ideas:

M's: manpower, materials, methods, money, management
P's: purpose, program, policy, plan, procedure, practice, problems, pitfalls, personnel, public relations

  a. Six basic steps in handling problems:
  1. Preliminary plan and background development
  2. Collect information, data and facts
  3. Analyze and interpret information, data and facts
  4. Analyze and develop solutions as well as make recommendations
  5. Prepare report and sell recommendations
  6. Install recommendations and follow up effectiveness

  b. Pitfalls to avoid
  1. *Taking things for granted* – A statement of the situation does not necessarily imply that each of the elements is necessarily true; for example, a complaint may be invalid and biased so that all that can be taken for granted is that a complaint has been registered

2. *Considering only one side of a situation* – Wherever possible, indicate several alternatives and then point out the reasons you selected the best one
3. *Failing to indicate follow up* – Whenever your answer indicates action on your part, make certain that you will take proper follow-up action to see how successful your recommendations, procedures or actions turn out to be
4. *Taking too long in answering any single question* – Remember to time your answers properly

IX. AFTER THE TEST

Scoring procedures differ in detail among civil service jurisdictions although the general principles are the same. Whether the papers are hand-scored or graded by machine we have described, they are nearly always graded by number. That is, the person who marks the paper knows only the number – never the name – of the applicant. Not until all the papers have been graded will they be matched with names. If other tests, such as training and experience or oral interview ratings have been given, scores will be combined. Different parts of the examination usually have different weights. For example, the written test might count 60 percent of the final grade, and a rating of training and experience 40 percent. In many jurisdictions, veterans will have a certain number of points added to their grades.

After the final grade has been determined, the names are placed in grade order and an eligible list is established. There are various methods for resolving ties between those who get the same final grade – probably the most common is to place first the name of the person whose application was received first. Job offers are made from the eligible list in the order the names appear on it. You will be notified of your grade and your rank as soon as all these computations have been made. This will be done as rapidly as possible.

People who are found to meet the requirements in the announcement are called "eligibles." Their names are put on a list of eligible candidates. An eligible's chances of getting a job depend on how high he stands on this list and how fast agencies are filling jobs from the list.

When a job is to be filled from a list of eligibles, the agency asks for the names of people on the list of eligibles for that job. When the civil service commission receives this request, it sends to the agency the names of the three people highest on this list. Or, if the job to be filled has specialized requirements, the office sends the agency the names of the top three persons who meet these requirements from the general list.

The appointing officer makes a choice from among the three people whose names were sent to him. If the selected person accepts the appointment, the names of the others are put back on the list to be considered for future openings.

That is the rule in hiring from all kinds of eligible lists, whether they are for typist, carpenter, chemist, or something else. For every vacancy, the appointing officer has his choice of any one of the top three eligibles on the list. This explains why the person whose name is on top of the list sometimes does not get an appointment when some of the persons lower on the list do. If the appointing officer chooses the second or third eligible, the No. 1 eligible does not get a job at once, but stays on the list until he is appointed or the list is terminated.

X. HOW TO PASS THE INTERVIEW TEST

The examination for which you applied requires an oral interview test. You have already taken the written test and you are now being called for the interview test – the final part of the formal examination.

You may think that it is not possible to prepare for an interview test and that there are no procedures to follow during an interview. Our purpose is to point out some things you can do in advance that will help you and some good rules to follow and pitfalls to avoid while you are being interviewed.

What is an interview supposed to test?

The written examination is designed to test the technical knowledge and competence of the candidate; the oral is designed to evaluate intangible qualities, not readily measured otherwise, and to establish a list showing the relative fitness of each candidate – as measured against his competitors – for the position sought. Scoring is not on the basis of "right" and "wrong," but on a sliding scale of values ranging from "not passable" to "outstanding." As a matter of fact, it is possible to achieve a relatively low score without a single "incorrect" answer because of evident weakness in the qualities being measured.

Occasionally, an examination may consist entirely of an oral test – either an individual or a group oral. In such cases, information is sought concerning the technical knowledges and abilities of the candidate, since there has been no written examination for this purpose. More commonly, however, an oral test is used to supplement a written examination.

Who conducts interviews?

The composition of oral boards varies among different jurisdictions. In nearly all, a representative of the personnel department serves as chairman. One of the members of the board may be a representative of the department in which the candidate would work. In some cases, "outside experts" are used, and, frequently, a businessman or some other representative of the general public is asked to serve. Labor and management or other special groups may be represented. The aim is to secure the services of experts in the appropriate field.

However the board is composed, it is a good idea (and not at all improper or unethical) to ascertain in advance of the interview who the members are and what groups they represent. When you are introduced to them, you will have some idea of their backgrounds and interests, and at least you will not stutter and stammer over their names.

What should be done before the interview?

While knowledge about the board members is useful and takes some of the surprise element out of the interview, there is other preparation which is more substantive. It *is* possible to prepare for an oral interview – in several ways:

1) Keep a copy of your application and review it carefully before the interview

This may be the only document before the oral board, and the starting point of the interview. Know what education and experience you have listed there, and the sequence and dates of all of it. Sometimes the board will ask you to review the highlights of your experience for them; you should not have to hem and haw doing it.

2) Study the class specification and the examination announcement

Usually, the oral board has one or both of these to guide them. The qualities, characteristics or knowledges required by the position sought are stated in these documents. They offer valuable clues as to the nature of the oral interview. For example, if the job involves supervisory responsibilities, the announcement will usually indicate that knowledge of modern supervisory methods and the qualifications of the candidate as a supervisor will be tested. If so, you can expect such questions, frequently in the form of a hypothetical situation which you are expected to solve. NEVER go into an oral without knowledge of the duties and responsibilities of the job you seek.

3) Think through each qualification required

Try to visualize the kind of questions you would ask if you were a board member. How well could you answer them? Try especially to appraise your own knowledge and background in each area, *measured against the job sought*, and identify any areas in which you are weak. Be critical and realistic – do not flatter yourself.

4) Do some general reading in areas in which you feel you may be weak

For example, if the job involves supervision and your past experience has NOT, some general reading in supervisory methods and practices, particularly in the field of human relations, might be useful. Do NOT study agency procedures or detailed manuals. The oral board will be testing your understanding and capacity, not your memory.

5) Get a good night's sleep and watch your general health and mental attitude

You will want a clear head at the interview. Take care of a cold or any other minor ailment, and of course, no hangovers.

What should be done on the day of the interview?

Now comes the day of the interview itself. Give yourself plenty of time to get there. Plan to arrive somewhat ahead of the scheduled time, particularly if your appointment is in the fore part of the day. If a previous candidate fails to appear, the board might be ready for you a bit early. By early afternoon an oral board is almost invariably behind schedule if there are many candidates, and you may have to wait. Take along a book or magazine to read, or your application to review, but leave any extraneous material in the waiting room when you go in for your interview. In any event, relax and compose yourself.

The matter of dress is important. The board is forming impressions about you – from your experience, your manners, your attitude, and your appearance. Give your personal appearance careful attention. Dress your best, but not your flashiest. Choose conservative, appropriate clothing, and be sure it is immaculate. This is a business interview, and your appearance should indicate that you regard it as such. Besides, being well groomed and properly dressed will help boost your confidence.

Sooner or later, someone will call your name and escort you into the interview room. *This is it.* From here on you are on your own. It is too late for any more preparation. But remember, you asked for this opportunity to prove your fitness, and you are here because your request was granted.

What happens when you go in?

The usual sequence of events will be as follows: The clerk (who is often the board stenographer) will introduce you to the chairman of the oral board, who will introduce you to the other members of the board. Acknowledge the introductions before you sit down. Do not be surprised if you find a microphone facing you or a stenotypist sitting by. Oral interviews are usually recorded in the event of an appeal or other review.

Usually the chairman of the board will open the interview by reviewing the highlights of your education and work experience from your application – primarily for the benefit of the other members of the board, as well as to get the material into the record. Do not interrupt or comment unless there is an error or significant misinterpretation; if that is the case, do not hesitate. But do not quibble about insignificant matters. Also, he will usually ask you some question about your education, experience or your present job – partly to get you to start talking and to establish the interviewing "rapport." He may start the actual questioning, or turn it over to one of the other members. Frequently, each member undertakes the questioning on a particular area, one in which he is perhaps most competent, so you can expect each member to participate in the examination. Because time is limited, you may also expect some rather abrupt switches in the direction the questioning takes, so do not be upset by it. Normally, a board member will not pursue a single line of questioning unless he discovers a particular strength or weakness.

After each member has participated, the chairman will usually ask whether any member has any further questions, then will ask you if you have anything you wish to add. Unless you are expecting this question, it may floor you. Worse, it may start you off on an extended, extemporaneous speech. The board is not usually seeking more information. The question is principally to offer you a last opportunity to present further qualifications or to indicate that you have nothing to add. So, if you feel that a significant qualification or characteristic has been overlooked, it is proper to point it out in a sentence or so. Do not compliment the board on the thoroughness of their examination – they have been sketchy, and you know it. If you wish, merely say, "No thank you, I have nothing further to add." This is a point where you can "talk yourself out" of a good impression or fail to present an important bit of information. Remember, *you close the interview yourself*.

The chairman will then say, "That is all, Mr. _____, thank you." Do not be startled; the interview is over, and quicker than you think. Thank him, gather your belongings and take your leave. Save your sigh of relief for the other side of the door.

How to put your best foot forward

Throughout this entire process, you may feel that the board individually and collectively is trying to pierce your defenses, seek out your hidden weaknesses and embarrass and confuse you. Actually, this is not true. They are obliged to make an appraisal of your qualifications for the job you are seeking, and they want to see you in your best light. Remember, they must interview all candidates and a non-cooperative candidate may become a failure in spite of their best efforts to bring out his qualifications. Here are 15 suggestions that will help you:

1) Be natural – Keep your attitude confident, not cocky

If you are not confident that you can do the job, do not expect the board to be. Do not apologize for your weaknesses, try to bring out your strong points. The board is interested in a positive, not negative, presentation. Cockiness will antagonize any board member and make him wonder if you are covering up a weakness by a false show of strength.

2) Get comfortable, but don't lounge or sprawl

Sit erectly but not stiffly. A careless posture may lead the board to conclude that you are careless in other things, or at least that you are not impressed by the importance of the occasion. Either conclusion is natural, even if incorrect. Do not fuss with your clothing, a pencil or an ashtray. Your hands may occasionally be useful to emphasize a point; do not let them become a point of distraction.

3) Do not wisecrack or make small talk

This is a serious situation, and your attitude should show that you consider it as such. Further, the time of the board is limited – they do not want to waste it, and neither should you.

4) Do not exaggerate your experience or abilities

In the first place, from information in the application or other interviews and sources, the board may know more about you than you think. Secondly, you probably will not get away with it. An experienced board is rather adept at spotting such a situation, so do not take the chance.

5) If you know a board member, do not make a point of it, yet do not hide it

Certainly you are not fooling him, and probably not the other members of the board. Do not try to take advantage of your acquaintanceship – it will probably do you little good.

6) Do not dominate the interview

Let the board do that. They will give you the clues – do not assume that you have to do all the talking. Realize that the board has a number of questions to ask you, and do not try to take up all the interview time by showing off your extensive knowledge of the answer to the first one.

7) Be attentive

You only have 20 minutes or so, and you should keep your attention at its sharpest throughout. When a member is addressing a problem or question to you, give him your undivided attention. Address your reply principally to him, but do not exclude the other board members.

8) Do not interrupt

A board member may be stating a problem for you to analyze. He will ask you a question when the time comes. Let him state the problem, and wait for the question.

9) Make sure you understand the question

Do not try to answer until you are sure what the question is. If it is not clear, restate it in your own words or ask the board member to clarify it for you. However, do not haggle about minor elements.

10) Reply promptly but not hastily

A common entry on oral board rating sheets is "candidate responded readily," or "candidate hesitated in replies." Respond as promptly and quickly as you can, but do not jump to a hasty, ill-considered answer.

11) Do not be peremptory in your answers

A brief answer is proper – but do not fire your answer back. That is a losing game from your point of view. The board member can probably ask questions much faster than you can answer them.

12) Do not try to create the answer you think the board member wants

He is interested in what kind of mind you have and how it works – not in playing games. Furthermore, he can usually spot this practice and will actually grade you down on it.

13) Do not switch sides in your reply merely to agree with a board member

Frequently, a member will take a contrary position merely to draw you out and to see if you are willing and able to defend your point of view. Do not start a debate, yet do not surrender a good position. If a position is worth taking, it is worth defending.

14) Do not be afraid to admit an error in judgment if you are shown to be wrong

The board knows that you are forced to reply without any opportunity for careful consideration. Your answer may be demonstrably wrong. If so, admit it and get on with the interview.

15) Do not dwell at length on your present job

The opening question may relate to your present assignment. Answer the question but do not go into an extended discussion. You are being examined for a *new* job, not your present one. As a matter of fact, try to phrase ALL your answers in terms of the job for which you are being examined.

Basis of Rating

Probably you will forget most of these "do's" and "don'ts" when you walk into the oral interview room. Even remembering them all will not ensure you a passing grade. Perhaps you did not have the qualifications in the first place. But remembering them will help you to put your best foot forward, without treading on the toes of the board members.

Rumor and popular opinion to the contrary notwithstanding, an oral board wants you to make the best appearance possible. They know you are under pressure – but they also want to see how you respond to it as a guide to what your reaction would be under the pressures of the job you seek. They will be influenced by the degree of poise you display, the personal traits you show and the manner in which you respond.

ABOUT THIS BOOK

This book contains tests divided into Examination Sections. Go through each test, answering every question in the margin. We have also attached a sample answer sheet at the back of the book that can be removed and used. At the end of each test look at the answer key and check your answers. On the ones you got wrong, look at the right answer choice and learn. Do not fill in the answers first. Do not memorize the questions and answers, but understand the answer and principles involved. On your test, the questions will likely be different from the samples. Questions are changed and new ones added. If you understand these past questions you should have success with any changes that arise. Tests may consist of several types of questions. We have additional books on each subject should more study be advisable or necessary for you. Finally, the more you study, the better prepared you will be. This book is intended to be the last thing you study before you walk into the examination room. Prior study of relevant texts is also recommended. NLC publishes some of these in our Fundamental Series. Knowledge and good sense are important factors in passing your exam. Good luck also helps. So now study this Passbook, absorb the material contained within and take that knowledge into the examination. Then do your best to pass that exam.

EXAMINATION SECTION

WORD MEANING
COMMENTARY

DESCRIPTION OF THE TEST
On many examinations, you will have questions about the meaning of words, or vocabulary.

In this type of question you have to state what a word or phrase means. (A phrase is a group of words.) This word or phrase is in CAPITAL letters in a sentence. You are also given for each question five other words or groups of words — lettered A, B, C, D, and E — as possible answers. One of thes words or groups of words means the same as the word or group of words in CAPITAL letters. Only one is right. You are to pick out the one that is right and select the letter of your answer.

HINTS FOR ANSWERING WORD-MEANING QUESTIONS
Read each question carefully.

Choose the best answer of the five choices even though it is not the word you might use yourself.

Answer first those that you know. Then do the others.

If you know that some of the suggested answers are not right, pay no more attention to them.

Be sure that you have selected an answer for every question, even if you have to guess.

SAMPLE QUESTIONS

DIRECTIONS: For the following questions, select the word or group of words lettered A, B, C, D, or E that means MOST NEARLY the same as the word in capital letters. Indicate the letter of the CORRECT answer for each question.

SAMPLE QUESTIONS 1 AND 2

1. The letter was SHORT. SHORT means *MOST NEARLY*

   A. tall   B. wide   C. brief   D. heavy   E. dark

   EXPLANATION
   SHORT is a word you have used to describe something that is small, or not long, or little, etc. Therefore you would not have to spend much time figuring out the right answer. You would choose C. brief.

2. The young man is VIGOROUS. VIGOROUS means *MOST NEARLY*

   A. serious   B. reliable   C. courageous
   D. strong   E. talented

   EXPLANATION
   VIGOROUS is a word that you have probably used yourself or read somewhere. It carries with it the idea of being active, full of pep, etc. Which one of the five choices comes closest to meaning that? Certainly not A. serious, B. reliable, or E. talented; C. courageous — maybe, D. strong — maybe. But between courageous or strong, you would have to agree that strong is the better choice. Therefore, you would choose D.

WORD MEANING

EXAMINATION SECTION
TEST 1

DIRECTIONS: Each question or incomplete statement is followed by several suggested answers or completions. Select the one that BEST answers the question or completes the statement. *PRINT THE LETTER OF THE CORRECT ANSWER IN THE SPACE AT HE IGHT.*

1. He received a large reward.
   In this sentence, the word *reward* means

   A. capture   B. recompense   C. key   D. praise

   1.____

2. The aide was asked to transmit a message. In this sentence, the word *transmit* means

   A. change   B. send   C. take   D. type

   2.____

3. The pest control aide requested the tenant to call the Health Department.
   In this sentence, the word *requested* means the pest control aide

   A. asked   B. helped   C. informed   D. warned

   3.____

4. The driver had to return the department's truck. In this sentence, the word *return* means

   A. borrow   B. fix   C. give back   D. load up

   4.____

5. The aide discussed the purpose of the visit. In this sentence, the word *purpose* means

   A. date   B. hour   C. need   D. reason

   5.____

6. The tenant suspected the aide who knocked at her door. In this sentence, the word *suspected* means

   A. answered   B. called   C. distrusted   D. welcomed

   6.____

7. The aide was positive that the child hit her. In this sentence, the word *positive* means

   A. annoyed   B. certain   C. sorry   D. surprised

   7.____

8. The tenant declined to call the Health Department. In this sentence, the word *declined* means

   A. agreed   B. decided   C. refused   D. wanted

   8.____

9. The porter cleaned the vacant room.
   In this sentence, the word *vacant* means NEARLY the same as

   A. empty   B. large   C. main   D. crowded

   9.____

10. The supervisor gave a brief report to his men.
    In this sentence, the word *brief* means NEARLY the same as

    A. long   B. safety   C. complete   D. short

    10.____

11. The supervisor told him to connect the two pieces.
    In this sentence, the word *connect* means NEARLY the same as

    A. join   B. paint   C. return   D. weigh

12. Standing on the top of a ladder is risky.
    In this sentence, the word *risky* means NEARLY the same as

    A. dangerous   B. sensible   C. safe   D. foolish

13. He raised the cover of the machine.
    In this sentence, the word *raised* means NEARLY the same as

    A. broke   B. lifted   C. lost   D. found

14. The form used for reporting the finished work was revised. In this sentence, the word *revised* means NEARLY the same as

    A. printed   B. ordered   C. dropped   D. changed

15. He did his work rapidly.
    In this sentence, the word *rapidly* means NEARLY the same a

    A. carefully   B. quickly   C. slowly   D. quietly

16. The worker was occasionally late.
    In this sentence, the word *occasionally* means NEARLY the same as

    A. sometimes   B. often   C. never   D. always

17. He selected the best tool for the job.
    In this sentence, the word *selected* means NEARLY the same as

    A. bought   B. picked   C. lost   D. broke

18. He needed assistance to lift the package.
    In this sentence, the word *assistance* means NEARLY the same as

    A. strength   B. time   C. help   D. instructions

19. The tools were issued by the supervisor.
    In this sentence, the word *issued* means NEARLY the same as

    A. collected   B. cleaned up   C. given out   D. examined

20. A permit for a tap for unmetered water will be issued only on prepayment of all charges for water to be used. In this sentence, the word *prepayment* means

    A. promise of payment   B. payment in advance
    C. payment as water is used   D. monthly payment

21. Upon application, the department will endeavor to locate a service pipe by means of an electrical indicator.
 In this sentence, the word *endeavor* means

 A. try B. help C. assist D. explore

22. It shall be unlawful for any person to operate certain equipment without previous permission from the department. In this sentence, the word *previous* means

 A. written B. oral C. prior D. provisional

23. All persons must comply with the rules and regulations. In this sentence, the word *comply* means

 A. agree B. coincide
 C. work carefully D. act in accord

24. No unauthorized person shall tamper with a water supply valve.
 In this sentence, the words *tamper with* means

 A. open B. operate C. alter D. shut

25. The use of water is permitted subject to such conditions as the department may consider reasonable.
 In this sentence, the word *reasonable* means

 A. necessary B. inexpensive C. fair D. desirable

26. An owner must engage a licensed plumber. In this sentence, the word *engage* means

 A. hire B. pay C. contact D. inform

27. The charges for a machine part are usually for the furnishing, delivering, and installing of the part. In this sentence, the word *furnishing* means

 A. preparing B. manufacturing C. finishing D. supplying

28. The investigator attempted to ascertain the facts.
 As used in this sentence, the word *ascertain* means MOST NEARLY to

 A. disprove B. find out C. go beyond D. explain

29. The speaker commenced the lecture with an anecdote.
 As used in this sentence, the word *commenced* means MOST NEARLY

 A. concluded B. illustrated C. enlivened D. started

30. The use of a hydrant may be authorized for construction purposes.
 As used in this sentence, the word *authorized* means

 A. possible B. permitted C. intended D. stopped

31. Conservation of the water supply is a major goal of the department.
    As used in this sentence, the word *conservation* means MOST NEARLY
    A. estimating
    B. increasing
    C. preserving
    D. purifying

32. Consumers should inspect their faucets frequently to guard against leaks.
    As used in this sentence, the word *consumers* means MOST NEARLY
    A. citizens
    B. owners
    C. producers
    D. users

33. The wire was connected to the adjacent terminal.
    As used in this sentence, the word *adjacent* means MOST NEARLY
    A. out of order
    B. metallic
    C. nearby
    D. negative

34. Some of the equipment supplied to the inspector was defective.
    As used in this sentence, the word *defective* means MOST NEARLY
    A. expensive
    B. faulty
    C. old
    D. unnecessary

35. The inspector was told to use discretion in dealing with the public.
    As used in this sentence, the word *discretion* means MOST NEARLY
    A. courtesy
    B. firmness
    C. judgment
    D. persuasion

36. It is unlawful to demolish any building without first obtaining a permit.
    As used in this sentence, the word *demolish* means MOST NEARLY
    A. build
    B. make alterations in
    C. occupy
    D. tear down

37. The clerk rendered an account of the cash received.
    As used in this sentence, the word *rendered* means MOST NEARLY
    A. concealed
    B. corrected
    C. forged
    D. gave

38. The permit was revoked by the department.
    As used in this sentence, the word *revoked* means MOST NEARLY
    A. approved
    B. cancelled
    C. renewed
    D. reviewed

39. The incident received much attention in the newspapers. As used in this sentence, the word *incident* means MOST NEARLY
    A. campaign
    B. crime
    C. event
    D. merger

40. The modification of the procedure was approved by the supervisor.
    As used in this sentence, the word *modification* means MOST NEARLY

    A. change B. interpretation
    C. repeal D. termination

41. The workers combined the contents of the two boxes. The word *combined* means

    A. sifted through B. put together
    C. tore apart   D. forgot about

42. Don't touch the lever on the left side. The word *lever* means

    A. button B. rope C. handle D. gun

43. All litter should be taken away. The word *litter* means

    A. paint B. bowls C. rubbish D. evidence

44. The inspection of the street was complete. The word *inspection* means

    A. cleaning B. examination
    C. repair   D. painting

45. The route must be followed exactly.
    The word *route* means

    A. foreman B. truck C. way D. recipe

46. Don't injure your back.
    The word *injure* means

    A. bend B. use C. hurt D. exercise

47. John repaired the machine.
    The word *repaired* means

    A. fixed B. broke C. ran D. oiled

48. Put the lid on the box.
    The word *lid* means

    A. cover B. ribbon C. rope D. wrapping

49. The rear of the truck should be washed.
    The word *rear* means

    A. hood B. front C. back D. roof

50. Coworkers must assist each other while at work. The word *assist* means

    A. help B. outdo C. like D. hurt

KEY (CORRECT ANSWERS)

1. B	11. A	21. A	31. C	41. B
2. B	12. A	22. C	32. D	42. C
3. A	13. B	23. D	33. C	43. C
4. C	14. D	24. C	34. B	44. B
5. D	15. B	25. C	35. C	45. C
6. C	16. A	26. A	36. D	46. C
7. B	17. B	27. D	37. D	47. A
8. C	18. C	28. B	38. B	48. A
9. A	19. C	29. D	39. C	49. C
10. D	20. B	30. B	40. A	50. A

TEST 2

DIRECTIONS: Each question or incomplete statement is followed by several suggested answers or completions. Select the one that BEST answers the question or completes the statement. *PRINT THE LETTER OF THE CORRECT ANSWER IN THE SPACE AT THE RIGHT.*

1. It is possible to construct a leak-proof home.
   The OPPOSITE of *construct* is

   A. build B. erect C. plant D. wreck

2. The driver had to repair the flat tire.
   The OPPOSITE of the word *repair* is

   A. destroy B. fix C. mend D. patch

3. The student tried to shout the answer.
   The OPPOSITE of the word *shout* is

   A. scream B. shriek C. whisper D. yell

4. Daily visits are the best.
   The OPPOSITE of the word *visits* is

   A. absences B. exercises C. lessons D. trials

5. It is important to arrive early in the morning.
   The OPPOSITE of the word *arrive* is

   A. climb B. descend C. enter D. leave

6. Mike is a group leader.
   The OPPOSITE of the word *leader* is

   A. boss B. chief C. follower D. overseer

7. The exterior of the house needs painting.
   The OPPOSITE of the word *exterior* is

   A. inside B. outdoors C. outside D. surface

8. He conceded the victory.
   The OPPOSITE of the word *conceded* is

   A. admitted B. denied C. granted D. reported

9. He watched the team begin.
   The OPPOSITE of the word *begin* is

   A. end B. fail C. gather D. win

10. Your handwriting is illegible.
    The OPPOSITE of the word *illegible* is

    A. clear B. confused C. jumbled D. unclear

11. The one of the following words that has the OPPOSITE meaning of *partition* is

    A. division   B. connection   C. barrier   D. compartment

12. The one of the following words that has the OPPOSITE meaning of *obvious* is

    A. concealed   B. known   C. clear   D. apparent

13. The one of the following words that has the OPPOSITE meaning of *assist* is

    A. hinder   B. offer   C. demand   D. aid

14. The one of the following words that has the OPPOSITE meaning of *obsolete* is

    A. neglected   B. traditional   C. rare   D. new

15. The one of the following words that has the OPPOSITE meaning of *stagnant* is

    A. murky   B. active   C. calm   D. dirty

16. The number of applicants exceeded the anticipated figure. As used in this sentence, the word *anticipated* means MOST NEARLY

    A. expected   B. required   C. revised   D. necessary

17. The clerk was told to collate the pages of the report. As used in this sentence, the word *collate* means MOST NEARLY

    A. destroy   B. edit   C. correct   D. assemble

18. Mr. Wells is not authorized to release the information. As used in this sentence, the word *authorized* means MOST NEARLY

    A. inclined   B. pleased   C. permitted   D. trained

19. The secretary chose an appropriate office for the meeting. As used in this sentence, the word *appropriate* means MOST NEARLY

    A. empty   B. decorated   C. nearby   D. suitable

20. The employee performs a complex set of tasks each day. As used in this sentence, the word *complex* means MOST NEARLY

    A. difficult   B. important   C. pleasant   D. large

21. In talking with a homeowner, an inspector should always be polite. As used in this sentence, the word *polite* means

    A. cold   B. courteous   C. aggressive   D. modest

22. In talking with a client, a worker should not discuss trivial matters. As used in this sentence, the word *trivial* means

    A. related   B. essential   C. significant   D. unimportant

23. The one of the following words that is SIMILAR in meaning to *revise* is

    A. edit   B. confuse   C. complicate   D. dismiss

24. The one of the following words that is SIMILAR in meaning to *abandon* is

    A. quit   B. use   C. remain   D. discourage

25. The one of the following words that is SIMILAR in meaning to *adjacent* is

    A. far   B. detached   C. bordering   D. distant

26. The one of the following words that is SIMILAR in meaning to *coarse* is

    A. fine   B. smooth   C. rough   D. slick

27. The one of the following words that is SIMILAR in meaning to *orifice* is

    A. chamber   B. enclosure   C. opening   D. device

28. The aide arrived on time.
    In this sentence, the word *arrived* means

    A. awoke   B. came   C. left   D. delayed

29. The salesman had to deliver books to each person he visited.
    In this sentence, the word *deliver* means

    A. give   B. lend   C. mail   D. sell

30. When estimating materials for interior plaster, consideration must be given to the number of coats.
    As used in this sentence, the word *estimating* means

    A. calculating approximately   B. purchasing
    C. mixing together   D. finishing

31. As used in the sentence in Question 30 above, the word *consideration* means

    A. extra weight   B. careful thought
    C. firmness   D. additions

32. When computing quantities of plaster for the scratch coat, no allowance may be made for the space occupied by the metal lath.
    As used in this sentence, the word *computing* means

    A. figuring   B. preparing   C. slaking   D. packing

33. As used in the sentence in Question 32 above, the word *allowance* means

    A. deduction   B. addition   C. leeway   D. closing

34. The supervisor made a ridiculous statement.
    As used in this sentence, the word *ridiculous* means MOST NEARLY

    A. incorrect   B. evil   C. unfriendly   D. foolish

35. That worker is engaged in a hazardous job.
    As used in this sentence, the word *hazardous* means MOST NEARLY

    A. inconvenient   B. dangerous   C. difficult   D. demanding

36. Breaks in water distribution mains are front page news for the very reason that they occur infrequently.
    As used in this sentence, the word *infrequently* means MOST NEARLY

    A. at regular intervals   B. often
    C. rarely   D. unexpectedly

37. Several kinds of self-caulking substitutes for lead have been developed.
    As used in this sentence, the word *substitutes* means MOST NEARLY

    A. additives   B. replacements   C. hardeners   D. softeners

38. Cast iron is essentially an alloy of iron and carbon. As used in this sentence, the word *essentially* means MOST NEARLY

    A. never   B. basically   C. barely   D. sometimes

39. When water moves through pipe, friction is developed between the water and the inside surface of the pipe. As used in this sentence, the word *friction* means MOST NEARLY

    A. resistance   B. heat   C. slippage   D. pressure

40. A person who is confident he can complete a task is said to be

    A. courageous   B. sure   C. bright   D. successful

41. If a child sleeping peacefully is awakened by a sudden cry, he is likely to be

    A. ill   B. uncomfortable   C. startled   D. hungry

42. He could not get his truck on the highway. A *highway* is a type of

    A. lot   B. road   C. scale   D. sidewalk

43. The large vehicle was being repaired.
    Which of the following is a *vehicle*?

    A. Truck   B. Building   C. Boiler   D. Table

44. The fence needs to be painted.
    The one of the following which is MOST like a *fence* is a

    A. door   B. crane   C. wall   D. building

45. Furniture is not taken with the regular garbage collection.
    Which of the following is *furniture*?

    A. Sofas and chairs   B. Cars and trucks
    C. Brooms and mops   D. Bags and boxes

46. The group was assigned to do special work. Which of the following is a *group*? 46._____

    A. Truck   B. Boat   C. Team   D. Foreman

47. Sanitation men often use tools in their work. 47._____
The one of the following which is MOST often considered a *tool* is a

    A. tire   B. shovel   C. glove   D. basket

48. The man claimed that he could not lift the box. The word *lift* means MOST NEARLY 48._____

    A. bury   B. pick up   C. refill   D. clean

49. Place all the boxes below the second shelf. The word *below* means 49._____

    A. under   B. into   C. beside   D. over

50. This street should be clean when the sanitation men finish. 50._____
The word *clean* means free of

    A. obstacles   B. pedestrians   C. traffic   D. dirt

KEY (CORRECT ANSWERS)

1. D	11. B	21. B	31. B	41. C
2. A	12. A	22. D	32. A	42. B
3. C	13. A	23. A	33. A	43. A
4. A	14. D	24. A	34. D	44. C
5. D	15. B	25. C	35. B	45. A
6. C	16. A	26. C	36. C	46. C
7. A	17. D	27. C	37. B	47. B
8. B	18. C	28. B	38. B	48. B
9. A	19. D	29. A	39. A	49. A
10. A	20. A	30. A	40. B	50. D

TEST 3

DIRECTIONS: Each question or incomplete statement is followed by several suggested answers or completions. Select the one that BEST answers the question or completes the statement. *PRINT THE LETTER OF THE CORRECT ANSWER IN THE SPACE AT THE RIGHT.*

Questions 1-6.

DIRECTIONS: In the paragraph below, some of the underlined words have been purposely changed and spoil the meaning that the rest of the paragraph is meant to give. Read the paragraph carefully. Then, answer Questions 1 through 6.

    The motor vehicle supervisor who is <u>responsible</u> for training drivers in the operation of <u>special</u> equipment cannot expect a man to carry out all of his duties <u>poorly</u> <u>immediately</u> after receiving instruction. The employee may be overwhelmed by all of the details he must master, <u>happy</u> because he is <u>associated</u> with new fellow workers, or fearful that he may not <u>succeed</u> on the job. It is the supervisor's <u>job</u> to make the <u>operator</u> feel at ease and <u>discourage</u> his self-confidence. The supervisor must also vary the speed of the <u>driving</u> according to the operator's <u>capacity</u> to <u>absorb</u> the instruction without undue pressure or confusion. All learners <u>progress</u> through <u>several</u> stages of <u>development</u> <u>unless</u> they become expert in their duties. As the operator's skills <u>increase,</u> he will require <u>more</u> instruction but the supervisor should be available to correct <u>mistakes</u> promptly to prevent wrong <u>habits</u> being formed.

1. Of the following words underlined in the above paragraph, the one that does NOT give the real meaning that the rest of the paragraph is meant to give is

    A. responsible   B. special   C. happy   D. immediately

2. Of the following words underlined in the above paragraph, the one that does NOT give the real meaning that the rest of the paragraph is meant to give is

    A. overwhelmed   B. happy   C. associated   D. succeed

3. Of the following words underlined in the above paragraph, the one that does NOT give the real meaning that the rest of the paragraph is meant to give is

    A. job   B. operator   C. discourage   D. self-confidence

4. Of the following words underlined in the above paragraph, the one that does NOT give the real meaning that the rest of the paragraph is meant to give is

    A. driving   B. capacity   C. absorb   D. pressure

5. Of the following words underlined in the above paragraph, the one that does NOT give the real meaning that the rest of the paragraph is meant to give is

    A. progress   B. several   C. development   D. unless

6. Of the following words underlined in the above paragraph, the one that does NOT give the real meaning that the rest of the paragraph is meant to give is

    A. increase   B. more   C. mistakes   D. habits

1.____

2.____

3.____

4.____

5.____

6.____

Questions 7-13.

DIRECTIONS: Each of Questions 7 through 13 consists of a capitalized word followed by four suggested meanings of the word. Select the word or phrase which means MOST NEARLY the same as the capitalized word.

7. ACCELERATE

   A. adjust B. press C. quicken D. strip

8. ALIGN

   A. bring into line B. carry out
   C. happen by chance D. join together

9. CONTRACTION

   A. agreement B. denial
   C. presentation D. shrinkage

10. INTERVAL

    A. ending B. mixing together of
    C. space of time D. weaken

11. LUBRICATE

    A. bend back B. make slippery
    C. rub out D. soften

12. OBSOLETE

    A. broken-down B. hard to find
    C. high-priced D. out of date

13. RETARD

    A. delay B. flatten C. rest D. tally

14. Any major components of a fire communication system should be meticulously maintained.
    In the preceding sentence, the word *meticulously* means MOST NEARLY

    A. indifferently B. perfunctorily
    C. painstakingly D. languidly

Questions 15-17.

DIRECTIONS: Questions 15 through 17 are to be answered in accordance with the following statement.

In order to facilitate prompt assembly of designated members, the officer in charge, Bureau of Fire Communications, shall maintain accurate current data on all such matters.

15. The word *facilitate,* as used in the above statement, means MOST NEARLY

    A. authorize   B. expedite   C. command   D. hinder

16. The word *designated,* as used in the above statement, means MOST NEARLY

    A. required   B. versatile   C. skillful   D. selected

17. The word *data,* as used in the above statement, means MOST NEARLY

    A. calculations   B. information   C. forecasts   D. surveillance

Questions 18-19.

DIRECTIONS: Questions 18 and 19 are to be answered in accordance with the following statement.

In the event of severe disruption of circuits....members of this squad may be.... detailed to Bureau of Fire Communications for duration of such emergency.

18. The word *disruption,* as used in the above sentence, means MOST NEARLY

    A. overloading   B. breakdown   C. disuse   D. concurrence

19. The word *detailed,* as used in the above statement, means MOST NEARLY

    A. assigned   B. reported   C. demoted   D. promoted

20. The officer in command, after verification that the alarm was false, shall transmit by radio the signal 9-2 followed by box number.
    The word *verification,* as used in the above sentence, means MOST NEARLY

    A. confirmation   B. consideration   C. notification   D. confutation

Questions 21-23.

DIRECTIONS: Questions 21 through 23 are to be answered on the basis of the following statement.

The manual of Fire Communications was planned to serve the Fire Department as guide and reference in effective use of its vast, versatile communications network.... Complete understanding of its phases and precepts, together with prompt compliance with all requirements and actions set in motion by its coded signals and radio transmissions, are essential.

21. The word *versatile,* as used in the above statement, means MOST NEARLY

    A. steady   B. many-sided   C. constant   D. wavering

22. The word *precepts,* as used in the above statement, means MOST NEARLY

    A. forerunners   B. paragraphs   C. rules   D. sections

23. The word *compliance,* as used in the above statement, means MOST NEARLY   23._____

    A. variance   B. dissension   C. divergence   D. conformance

24. A person who is influenced in making a decision by preconceived opinions is said to be   24._____

    A. subjective   B. obstinate   C. hateful   D. ignorant

25. No time was set for the conference.   25._____
    The word below that BEST describes this fact is

    A. indefinite   B. decisive   C. ignored   D. powerful

26. The truck could not go under the bridge because the bridge was too low.   26._____
    The reason the truck could not go under the bridge was that the bridge was not _____ enough.

    A. high   B. long   C. strong   D. wide

Questions 27-29.

DIRECTIONS: Questions 27 through 29 are to be answered on the basis of the following statement.

In structures exceeding 150 ft. in height, adequate means shall be provided for taking care of the expansion and contraction of all vertical lines of pipe. In addition, adequate means shall be provided to properly support all vertical lines of pipe.

27. The word *adequate,* as used above, means MOST NEARLY   27._____

    A. liquid devices
    B. properly designed and sufficient
    C. strong and thick walled
    D. in very great numbers

28. The word *expansion,* as used above, means MOST NEARLY a(n)   28._____

    A. bulbous swelling
    B. transverse projection
    C. large increase in diameter
    D. an increase in length

29. The word *contraction,* as used above, means MOST NEARLY   29._____

    A. contract to install the vertical line
    B. reduction in length
    C. to group all vertical lines together
    D. to decrease the equivalent length

30. A common mistake is to assume that the strength of equipment is the most important factor.   30._____
    As used in the above sentence, the word *assume* means MOST NEARLY

    A. determine   B. take for granted
    C. figure   D. make sure

KEY (CORRECT ANSWERS)

1. C	11. B	21. B
2. B	12. D	22. C
3. C	13. A	23. D
4. A	14. C	24. A
5. D	15. B	25. A
6. B	16. D	26. A
7. C	17. B	27. B
8. A	18. B	28. D
9. D	19. A	29. B
10. C	20. A	30. B

WORD MEANING
EXAMINATION SECTION
TEST 1

DIRECTIONS: Each question or incomplete statement is followed by several suggested answers or completions. Select the one that BEST answers the question or completes the statement. *PRINT THE LETTER OF THE CORRECT ANSWER IN THE SPACE AT THE RIGHT.*

1. He implied that he would work overtime if necessary.
   In this sentence, the word *implied* means

   A. denied
   B. explained
   C. guaranteed
   D. hinted

   1.____

2. The bag of the vacuum cleaner was inflated.
   In this sentence, the word *inflated* means

   A. blown up with air
   B. filled with dirt
   C. loose
   D. torn

   2.____

3. Burning material during certain hours is prohibited.
   In this sentence, the word *prohibited* means

   A. allowed   B. forbidden   C. legal   D. required

   3.____

4. He was rejected when he applied for the job. In this sentence, the word *rejected* means

   A. discouraged
   B. put to work
   C. tested
   D. turned down

   4.____

5. The foreman was able to substantiate his need for extra supplies.
   In this sentence, the word *substantiate* means

   A. estimate   B. meet   C. prove   D. reduce

   5.____

6. The new instructions supersede the old ones.
   In this sentence, the word *supersede* means

   A. explain   B. improve   C. include   D. replace

   6.____

7. Shake the broom free of surplus water and hang it up to dry.
   In this sentence, the word *surplus* means

   A. dirty   B. extra   C. rinse   D. soapy

   7.____

8. When a crack is filled, the asphalt must be tamped.
   In this sentence, the word *tamped* means

   A. cured
   B. heated
   C. packed down
   D. wet down

   8.____

9. The apartment was left vacant.
   In this sentence, the word *vacant* means

   A. clean   B. empty   C. furnished   D. locked

   9.____

10. The caretaker spent the whole day doing various repairs.
    In this sentence, the word *various* means

    A. different   B. necessary   C. small   D. special

11. He came back to assist his partner.
    In this sentence, the word *assist* means

    A. call   B. help   C. stop   D. question

12. A person who is biased cannot be a good foreman.
    In this sentence, the word *biased* means

    A. easy-going   B. prejudiced
    C. strict   D. uneducated

13. The lecture for the new employees was brief.
    In this sentence, the word *brief* means

    A. educational   B. free
    C. interesting   D. short

14. He was asked to clarify the order.
    In this sentence, the word *clarify* means

    A. follow out   B. make clear
    C. take back   D. write out

15. The employee was commended by his foreman.
    In this sentence, the word *commended* means

    A. assigned   B. blamed   C. picked   D. praised

16. Before the winter, the lawnmower engine was dismantled.
    In this sentence, the word *dismantled* means

    A. oiled   B. repaired
    C. stored away   D. taken apart

17. They excavated a big hole on the project lawn.
    In this sentence, the word *excavated* means

    A. cleaned out   B. discovered
    C. dug out   D. filled in

18. The new man was told to sweep the exterior area.
    In this sentence, the word *exterior* means

    A. asphalt   B. nearby   C. outside   D. whole

19. The officer refuted the statement of the driver.
    As used in this sentence, the word *refuted* means MOST NEARLY

    A. disproved   B. elaborated upon
    C. related   D. supported

20. The mechanism of the parking meter is not intricate.
    As used in this sentence, the word *intricate* means MOST NEARLY

    A. cheap   B. complicated
    C. foolproof   D. strong

21. The weight of each box fluctuates.
    As used in this sentence, the word *fluctuates* means MOST NEARLY

    A. always changes   B. decreases
    C. increases gradually   D. is similar

22. The person chosen to investigate the new procedure should be impartial.
    As used in this sentence, the word *impartial* means MOST NEARLY

    A. experienced   B. fair
    C. forward looking   D. important

23. Carelessness in the safekeeping of keys will not be tolerated.
    As used in this sentence, the word *tolerated* means MOST NEARLY

    A. forgotten   B. permitted
    C. punished lightly   D. understood

24. The traffic was easily diverted.
    As used in this sentence, the word *diverted* means MOST NEARLY

    A. controlled   B. speeded up
    C. stopped   D. turned aside

25. A transcript of the report was prepared in the office.
    As used in this sentence, the word *transcript* means MOST NEARLY

    A. brief   B. copy
    C. record   D. translation

26. The change was authorized by the supervisor.
    As used in this sentence, the word *authorized* means MOST NEARLY

    A. completed   B. corrected   C. ordered   D. permitted

27. The supervisor read the excerpt of the collector's report.
    According to this sentence, the supervisor read _____ the report.

    A. a passage from   B. a summary of
    C. the original of   D. the whole of

28. During the probation period, the worker proved to be inept.
    The word *inept* means MOST NEARLY

    A. incompetent   B. insubordinate
    C. satisfactory   D. uncooperative

29. The putative father was not living with the family.
    The word *putative* means MOST NEARLY

    A. reputed   B. unemployed
    C. concerned   D. indifferent

30. The adopted child researched various documents of vital statistics in an effort to discover the names of his natural parents.
    The words *vital statistics* mean MOST NEARLY statistics relating to

    A. human life
    B. hospitals
    C. important facts
    D. health and welfare

31. Despite many requests for them, there was a scant supply of new blotters.
    The word *scant* means MOST NEARLY

    A. adequate
    B. abundant
    C. insufficient
    D. expensive

32. Did they replenish the supply of forms in the cabinet?
    The word *replenish* means MOST NEARLY

    A. straighten up
    B. refill
    C. sort out
    D. use

33. Employees may become bored if they are assigned diverse duties.
    The word *diverse* means MOST NEARLY

    A. interesting
    B. different
    C. challenging
    D. enjoyable

Questions 34-37.

DIRECTIONS: Each of Questions 34 through 37 consists of a capitalized word followed by four suggested meanings of the word. Select the word or phrase which means MOST NEARLY the same as the capitalized word.

34. PROFICIENCY

    A. vocation
    B. competency
    C. repugnancy
    D. prominence

35. BIBLIOGRAPHY

    A. description
    B. stenography
    C. photograph
    D. compilation of books

36. FIDELITY

    A. belief
    B. treachery
    C. strength
    D. loyalty

37. ACCELERATE

    A. adjust   B. press   C. quicken   D. strip

38. One of the machinists in your shop enjoys the reputation of being a great equivocator.
    This means MOST NEARLY that he

    A. takes pride and is happy in his work
    B. generally hedges and often gives misleading answers
    C. is a strong union man with great interest in his fellow workers' welfare
    D. is good at resolving disputes

39. When a person has the reputation of persistently making foolish or silly remarks, it may be said that he is

   A. inane
   B. meticulous
   C. a procrastinator
   D. a prevaricator

40. When two mechanics, called A and B, make measurements of the same workpiece and find significant discrepancies in their measurements, it is MOST NEARLY correct to state that

   A. mechanic B made an erroneous reading
   B. mechanic A was careless in making his measurements
   C. both mechanics made their measurements correctly
   D. there was considerable difference in the two sets of measurements

41. A foreman who *expedites* a job,

   A. abolishes it
   B. makes it bigger
   C. slows it down
   D. speeds it up

42. If a man is working at a *uniform* speed, it means he is working at a speed which is

   A. changing
   B. fast
   C. slow
   D. steady

43. To say that a caretaker is *obstinate* means that he is

   A. cooperative
   B. patient
   C. stubborn
   D. willing

44. To say that a caretaker is *negligent* means that he is

   A. careless
   B. neat
   C. nervous
   D. late

45. To say that something is *absurd* means that it is

   A. definite
   B. not clear
   C. ridiculous
   D. unfair

46. To say that a foreman is *impartial* means that he is

   A. fair
   B. improving
   C. in a hurry
   D. watchful

47. A man who is *lenient* is one who is

   A. careless
   B. harsh
   C. inexperienced
   D. mild

48. A man who is *punctual* is one who is

   A. able
   B. polite
   C. prompt
   D. sincere

49. If you think one of your men is too *awkward* to do a job, it means you think he is too

   A. clumsy
   B. lazy
   C. old
   D. weak

50. A person who is *seldom* late, is late

   A. always
   B. never
   C. often
   D. rarely

KEY (CORRECT ANSWERS)

1. D	11. B	21. A	31. C	41. D
2. A	12. B	22. B	32. B	42. D
3. B	13. D	23. B	33. B	43. C
4. D	14. B	24. D	34. B	44. A
5. C	15. D	25. B	35. D	45. C
6. D	16. D	26. D	36. D	46. A
7. B	17. C	27. A	37. C	47. D
8. C	18. C	28. A	38. B	48. C
9. B	19. A	29. A	39. B	49. A
10. A	20. B	30. A	40. D	50. D

TEST 2

DIRECTIONS: Each question or incomplete statement is followed by several suggested answers or completions. Select the one that BEST answers the question or completes the statement. *PRINT THE LETTER OF THE CORRECT ANSWER IN THE SPACE AT THE RIGHT.*

1. The Department of Health can certify that conditions in a housing accommodation are detrimental to life or health.
   As used in the above sentence, the word *detrimental* means MOST NEARLY

   A. injurious B. serious
   C. satisfactory D. necessary

2. The Administrator shall have the power to revoke any adjustment in rents granted either the landlord or the tenant.
   As used in the above sentence, the word *revoke* means MOST NEARLY

   A. increase B. decrease C. rescind D. restore

Questions 3-5.

DIRECTIONS: Each of Questions 3 through 5 consists of a capitalized word followed by four suggested meanings of the word. Select the word which means MOST NEARLY the same as the capitalized word.

3. DOGMATISM

   A. dramatism B. positiveness
   C. doubtful D. tentativeness

4. ELECTRODE

   A. officer B. electrolyte
   C. terminal D. positive

5. EMIT

   A. return B. enter C. omit D. discharge

6. The word *inflammable* means MOST NEARLY

   A. burnable B. acid C. poisonous D. explosive

7. The word *disinfect* means MOST NEARLY

   A. deodorize B. sterilize C. bleach D. dissolve

8. He wanted to ascertain the facts before arriving at a conclusion.
   The word *ascertain* means MOST NEARLY

   A. disprove B. determine C. convert D. provide

9. Did the supervisor assent to her request for annual leave?
   The word *assent* means MOST NEARLY

   A. allude B. protest C. agree D. refer

10. The new worker was fearful that the others would rebuff her.
    The word *rebuff* means MOST NEARLY

    A. ignore   B. forget   C. copy   D. snub

11. The supervisor of that office does not condone lateness.
    The word *condone* means MOST NEARLY

    A. mind   B. excuse   C. punish   D. remember

12. Each employee was instructed to be as concise as possible when preparing a report.
    The word *concise* means MOST NEARLY

    A. exact   B. sincere   C. flexible   D. brief

13. The shovelers should not distribute the asphalt faster than it can be properly handled by the rakers.
    As used above, *distribute* means MOST NEARLY

    A. dump   B. pick-up   C. spread   D. heat

14. Any defective places should be cut out.
    As used above, *defective* means MOST NEARLY

    A. low   B. hard   C. soft   D. faulty

15. *Sphere of authority* is called

    A. constituency   B. dictatorial
    C. jurisdiction   D. vassal

16. Rollers are made in several sizes.
    As used above, *several* means MOST NEARLY

    A. large   B. heavy   C. standard   D. different

17. Sometimes a roller is run over an old surface to detect weak spots.
    As used above, *detect* means MOST NEARLY

    A. compact   B. remove   C. find   D. strengthen

18. Reconstruction of the old base is sometimes required as a preliminary operation.
    As used above, *preliminary* means MOST NEARLY

    A. first   B. necessary   C. important   D. local

19. If a man makes an *absurd* remark, he makes one which is MOST NEARLY

    A. misleading   B. ridiculous
    C. unfair   D. wicked

20. A worker who is *adept* at his job is one who is MOST NEARLY

    A. cooperative   B. developed
    C. diligent   D. skilled

21. If a man states a condition is *general,* he means it is MOST NEARLY

    A. artificial   B. prevalent
    C. timely   D. transient

Questions 22-50.

DIRECTIONS: Each of Questions 22 through 50 consists of a sentence in which a word is italicized. Of the four words following each sentence, select the word whose meaning is MOST NEARLY the same as the meaning of the italicized word.

22. The agent's first *assignment* was to patrol on Hicks Avenue.

    A. test B. sign C. job D. deadline

23. Agents get many *inquiries* from the public.

    A. complaints B. suggestions
    C. compliments D. questions

24. The names of all fifty states were written in *abbreviated* form.

    A. shortened B. corrected
    C. eliminated D. illegible

25. The meter was examined and found to be *defective*.

    A. small B. operating C. destroyed D. faulty

26. Agent Roger's reports are *legible,* but Agent Baldwin's are not.

    A. similar B. readable C. incorrect D. late

27. The time allowed, as shown by the meter, had *expired*.

    A. started B. broken C. ended D. violated

28. The busy *commercial* area is quiet in the evenings.

    A. deserted B. growing C. business D. local

29. The district office *authorized* the giving of summonses to illegally parked trucks.

    A. suggested B. approved
    C. prohibited D. recorded

30. Department property must be used *exclusively* for official business.

    A. occasionally B. frequently
    C. only D. properly

31. The District Commander *banned* driving in the area.

    A. detoured B. permitted
    C. encouraged D. prohibited

32. Two copies of the summons are *retained* by the Enforcement Agent.

    A. kept B. distributed
    C. submitted D. signed

33. The Agent *detected* a parking violation.

    A. cancelled B. discovered
    C. investigated D. reported

34. *Pedestrians* may be given summonses for violating traffic regulations.
    A. Bicycle riders
    B. Horsemen
    C. Motorcyclists
    D. Walkers

35. Parked cars are not allowed to *obstruct* traffic.
    A. direct
    B. lead
    C. block
    D. speed

36. It was *obvious* to the Agent that the traffic light was broken.
    A. uncertain
    B. surprising
    C. possible
    D. clear

37. The signs stated that parking in the area was *restricted* to vehicles of foreign diplomats.
    A. allowed
    B. increased
    C. desired
    D. limited

38. Each violation carries an *appropriate* fine.
    A. suitable
    B. extra
    C. light
    D. heavy

39. Strict enforcement of parking regulations helps to *alleviate* traffic congestion.
    A. extend
    B. build
    C. relieve
    D. increase

40. The Bureau has a rule which states that an Agent shall speak and act *courteously* in any relationship with the public.
    A. respectfully
    B. timidly
    C. strangely
    D. intelligently

41. City traffic regulations prohibit parking at *jammed* meters.
    A. stuck
    B. timed
    C. open
    D. installed

42. A *significant* error was made by the collector.
    A. doubtful
    B. foolish
    C. important
    D. strange

43. It is better to *disperse* a crowd.
    A. hold back
    B. quiet
    C. scatter
    D. talk to

44. Business groups wish to *expand* the program.
    A. advertise
    B. defeat
    C. enlarge
    D. expose

45. The procedure was *altered* to assist the storekeepers.
    A. abolished
    B. changed
    C. improved
    D. made simpler

46. The collector was instructed to *survey* the damage to the parking meter.
    A. examine
    B. give the reason for
    C. repair
    D. report

47. It is *imperative* that a collector's report be turned in after each collection.
    A. desired
    B. recommended
    C. requested
    D. urgent

48. The collector was not able to *extricate* the key.

    A. find
    B. free
    C. have a copy made of
    D. turn

49. Parking meters have *alleviated* one of our major traffic problems.

    A. created
    B. lightened
    C. removed
    D. solved

50. Formerly drivers with learners' permits could drive only on *designated* streets.

    A. dead-end   B. not busy   C. one way   D. specified

KEY (CORRECT ANSWERS)

1. A	11. B	21. B	31. D	41. A
2. C	12. D	22. C	32. A	42. C
3. B	13. C	23. D	33. B	43. C
4. C	14. D	24. A	34. D	44. C
5. D	15. C	25. D	35. C	45. B
6. A	16. D	26. B	36. D	46. A
7. B	17. C	27. C	37. D	47. D
8. B	18. A	28. C	38. A	48. B
9. C	19. B	29. B	39. C	49. B
10. D	20. D	30. C	40. A	50. D

TEST 3

DIRECTIONS: Each question or incomplete statement is followed by several suggested answers or completions. Select the one that BEST answers the question or completes the statement. *PRINT THE LETTER OF THE CORRECT ANSWER IN THE SPACE AT THE RIGHT.*

1. Sprinkler systems in buildings can retard the spread of fires.
   As used in this sentence, the word *retard* means MOST NEARLY

   A. quench   B. slow   C. reveal   D. aggravate

2. Although there was widespread criticism, the director refused to curtail the program.
   As used in this sentence, the word *curtail* means MOST NEARLY

   A. change   B. discuss   C. shorten   D. expand

3. Argon is an inert gas.
   As used in this sentence, the word *inert* means MOST NEARLY

   A. unstable   B. uncommon   C. volatile   D. inactive

4. The firemen turned their hoses on the shed and the main building simultaneously.
   As used in this sentence, the word *simultaneously* means MOST NEARLY

   A. in turn
   B. without hesitation
   C. with great haste
   D. at the same time

5. The officer was rebuked for his failure to act promptly. As used in this sentence, the word *rebuked* means MOST NEARLY

   A. demoted
   B. reprimanded
   C. discharged
   D. reassigned

6. Parkways in the city may be used to facilitate responses to fire alarms.
   As used in this sentence, the word *facilitate* means MOST NEARLY

   A. reduce   B. alter   C. complete   D. ease

7. Fire extinguishers are most effective when the fire is incipient.
   As used in this sentence, the word *incipient* means MOST NEARLY

   A. accessible
   B. beginning
   C. red hot
   D. confined

8. It is important to convey to new members the fundamentals of the procedure.
   As used in this sentence, the words *convey to* means MOST NEARLY

   A. prove for
   B. confirm for
   C. suggest to
   D. impart to

9. The explosion was a graphic illustration of the effects of neglect and carelessness.
   As used in this sentence, the word *graphic* means MOST NEARLY

   A. terrible   B. typical   C. unique   D. vivid

10. The worker was assiduous in all things relating to his duties.
    As used in this sentence, the word *assiduous* means MOST NEARLY

    A. aggressive   B. careless   C. persistent   D. cautious

11. A worker must be adept to be successful at his work.
    As used in this sentence, the word *adept* means MOST NEARLY

    A. ambitious   B. strong   C. agile   D. skillful

12. The extinguisher must be inverted before it will operate. As used in this sentence, the word *inverted* means MOST NEARLY

    A. turned over   B. completely filled
    C. lightly shaken   D. unhooked

13. Assume that the bridge operator may at times be assigned to the task of coordinating the bridge crew for the various routine jobs.
    As used in this sentence, the word *coordinating* means MOST NEARLY

    A. ordering   B. testing
    C. scheduling   D. instructing

14. The worker made an insignificant error.
    As used in this sentence, the word *insignificant* means MOST NEARLY

    A. latent   B. serious
    C. accidental   D. minor

15. An Assistant Supervisor should be attentive.
    As used in this sentence, the word *attentive* means MOST NEARLY

    A. watchful   B. prompt   C. negligent   D. willing

16. The Assistant Supervisor reported a cavity in the roadway.
    As used in this sentence, the word *cavity* means MOST NEARLY

    A. lump   B. wreck   C. hollow   D. oil-slick

17. Anyone working in traffic must be cautious.
    As used in this sentence, the word *cautious* means MOST NEARLY

    A. brave   B. careful   C. expert   D. fast

Questions 18-20.

DIRECTIONS: Each of Questions 18 through 20 consists of a capitalized word followed by four suggested meanings of the word. Select the word or phrase which means MOST NEARLY the same as the capitalized word.

18. OSMOSIS

    A. combining   B. diffusion
    C. ossification   D. incantation

19. COLLOIDAL

    A. mucinous   B. powdered   C. hairy   D. beautiful

20. PRETEXT
    A. ritual
    B. fictitious reason
    C. sermon
    D. truthful motive

21. *Easily broken or snapped* defines the word
    A. brittle   B. pliable   C. cohesive   D. volatile

22. *At right angles to a given line or surface* defines the word
    A. horizontal
    B. oblique
    C. perpendicular
    D. adjacent

23. *Tools with cutting edges for enlarging or shaping holes* are
    A. screwdrivers
    B. pliers
    C. reamers
    D. nippers

24. *An instrument used for measuring very small distances* is called a
    A. gage
    B. compass
    C. slide ruler
    D. micrometer

25. When the phrase *acrid smoke* is used, it refers to smoke that is
    A. irritating
    B. dense
    C. black
    D. very hot

26. The officer gave explicit directions on how the work was to be done.
    As used in this sentence, the word *explicit* means MOST NEARLY
    A. implied   B. clear   C. vague   D. brief

27. After the fire had been extinguished, the debris was taken outside and soaked.
    As used in this sentence, the word *debris* means MOST NEARLY
    A. wood   B. rubbish   C. couch   D. paper

28. The trapped man blanched when he saw the life net below him.
    As used in this sentence, the word *blanched* means MOST NEARLY
    A. turned pale
    B. sprang forward
    C. flushed
    D. fainted

29. The worker and his supervisor discussed the problem candidly.
    As used in this sentence, the word *candidly* means MOST NEARLY
    A. angrily
    B. frankly
    C. tolerantly
    D. understandingly

30. The truck came careening down the street.
    As used in this sentence, the word *careening* means MOST NEARLY
    A. with sirens screaming
    B. at a slow speed
    C. swaying from side to side
    D. out of control

31. The population of the province is fairly homogeneous.
    As used in this sentence, the word *homogeneous* means MOST NEARLY

    A. devoted to agricultural pursuits
    B. conservative in outlook
    C. essentially alike
    D. sophisticated

32. The reports of injuries during the past month are being tabulated.
    As used in this sentence, the word *tabulated* means MOST NEARLY

    A. analyzed
    B. placed in a file
    C. put in the form of a table
    D. verified

33. The terms offered were tantamount to surrender.
    As used in this sentence, the word *tantamount* means MOST NEARLY

    A. equivalent   B. opposite
    C. preferable   D. preliminary

34. The man's injuries were superficial.
    As used in this sentence, the word *superficial* means MOST NEARLY

    A. on the surface   B. not fatal
    C. free from infection D. not painful

35. This experience warped his outlook on life.
    As used in this sentence, the word *warped* means MOST NEARLY

    A. changed   B. improved
    C. strengthened   D. twisted

36. Hotel guests usually are transients.
    As used in this sentence, the word *transients* means MOST NEARLY

    A. persons of considerable wealth
    B. staying for a short time
    C. visitors from other areas
    D. untrustworthy persons

37. The pupil's work specimen was considered unsatisfactory because of his failure to observe established tolerances. As used in this sentence, the word *tolerances* means MOST NEARLY

    A. safety precautions
    B. regard for the rights of others
    C. allowable variations in dimensions
    D. amount of waste produced in an operation

38. Punishment was severe because the act was considered willful.
    As used in this sentence, the word *willful* means MOST NEARLY

    A. brutal   B. criminal
    C. harmful   D. intentional

39. The malfunctioning of the system was traced to a defective thermostat.
    As used in this sentence, the word *thermostat* means MOST NEARLY a device that reacts to changes in

    A. amperage
    B. water pressure
    C. temperature
    D. atmospheric pressure

40. His garden contained a profusion of flowers, shrubs, and bushes.
    As used in this sentence, the word *profusion* means MOST NEARLY

    A. abundance
    B. display
    C. representation
    D. scarcity

41. The inspector would not approve the work because it was out of plumb.
    As used in this sentence, the words *out of plumb* means MOST NEARLY not

    A. properly seasoned
    B. of the required strength
    C. vertical
    D. fireproof

42. The judge admonished the witness for his answer.
    As used in this sentence, the word *admonished* means MOST NEARLY

    A. complimented
    B. punished
    C. questioned
    D. warned

43. A millimeter is a measure of length.
    The length represented by *one millimeter* is

    A. one-thousandth of a meter
    B. one thousand meters
    C. one-millionth of a meter
    D. one million meters

44. It is not possible to misconstrue his letter.
    As used in this sentence, the word *misconstrue* means MOST NEARLY

    A. decipher
    B. forget
    C. ignore
    D. misinterpret

45. The wire connecting the two terminals must be kept taut.
    As used in this sentence, the word *taut* means MOST NEARLY without

    A. defects
    B. slack
    C. electrical charge
    D. pressure

46. Reaching the summit appeared beyond the capacity of the hikers.
    As used in this sentence, the word *summit* means MOST NEARLY

    A. canyon   B. peak   C. plateau   D. ravine

47. The plot was thwarted by the quick action of the police. As used in this sentence, the word *thwarted* means MOST NEARLY

    A. blocked
    B. discovered
    C. punished
    D. solved

48. An abrasive was required by the machinist to complete his task. 48.____
    As used in this sentence, the word *abrasive* means a substance used for

    A. coating
    B. lubricating
    C. measuring
    D. polishing

49. The facades of the building were dirty and grimy. 49.____
    As used in this sentence, the word *facades* means MOST NEARLY

    A. cellars
    B. fronts
    C. residents
    D. surroundings

50. Several firemen were injured by the detonation. 50.____
    As used in this sentence, the word *detonation* means MOST NEARLY

    A. accident   B. collapse   C. collision   D. explosion

KEY (CORRECT ANSWERS)

1. B	11. D	21. A	31. C	41. C
2. C	12. A	22. C	32. C	42. D
3. D	13. C	23. C	33. A	43. A
4. D	14. D	24. D	34. A	44. D
5. B	15. A	25. A	35. D	45. B
6. D	16. C	26. B	36. B	46. B
7. B	17. B	27. B	37. C	47. A
8. D	18. B	28. A	38. D	48. D
9. D	19. A	29. B	39. C	49. B
10. C	20. B	30. C	40. A	50. D

WORD MEANING
EXAMINATION SECTION
TEST 1

DIRECTIONS: Each question or incomplete statement is followed by several suggested answers or completions. Select the one that BEST answers the question or completes the statement. *PRINT THE LETTER OF THE CORRECT ANSWER IN THE SPACE AT THE RIGHT.*

1. Rules must be applied with discretion.
   As used in this sentence, the word *discretion* means MOST NEARLY

   A. impartiality   B. judgment
   C. severity   D. patience

2. The officer and his men ascended the stairs as rapidly as they could.
   As used in this sentence, the word *ascended* means MOST NEARLY

   A. went up   B. washed down
   C. chopped   D. shored up

3. The store's refusal to accept delivery of the merchandise was a violation of the express provisions of the contract. As used in this sentence, the word *express* means MOST NEARLY

   A. clear   B. implied   C. penalty   D. disputed

4. He needed public assistance because he was incapacitated. As used in this sentence, the word *incapacitated* means MOST NEARLY

   A. uneducated   B. disabled
   C. uncooperative D. discharged

5. The worker explained to the client that signing the document was compulsory.
   As used in this sentence, the word *compulsory* means MOST NEARLY

   A. temporary   B. required
   C. different   D. comprehensive

6. The woman's actions did not jeopardize her eligibility for benefits.
   As used in this sentence, the word *jeopardize* means MOST NEARLY

   A. delay   B. reinforce   C. determine   D. endanger

7. The cause of the emergency was a defective gas flue.
   As used in this sentence, the word *flue* means MOST NEARLY

   A. burner   B. duct   C. jet   D. supply

8. The crux of the matter is finding the right man for the job.
   As used in this sentence, the word *crux* means MOST NEARLY

   A. obvious solution   B. neglected consideration
   C. final step   D. decisive point

9. His assistance in this project was invaluable.
   As used in this sentence, the word *invaluable* means MOST NEARLY

   A. worthless
   B. priceless
   C. inconspicuous
   D. difficult to evaluate

10. There are many facets to this problem.
    As used in this sentence, the word *facets* means MOST NEARLY

    A. alternatives
    B. aspects
    C. difficulties
    D. solutions

11. The map clearly indicated the contour of the lake.
    As used in this sentence, the word *contour* means MOST NEARLY

    A. composition
    B. location
    C. outline
    D. source

12. The hot weather made him lethargic.
    As used in this sentence, the word *lethargic* means MOST NEARLY

    A. drowsy
    B. perspire
    C. tense
    D. thirsty

13. The arrangements for the meeting were haphazard.
    As used in this sentence, the word *haphazard* means MOST NEARLY

    A. according to a plan
    B. determined by mere chance
    C. overly detailed
    D. disregarded

14. The committee could not agree on an agenda for the conference.
    As used in this sentence, the word *agenda* means MOST NEARLY

    A. rules of procedure
    B. meeting place
    C. qualifications of delegates
    D. things to be done

15. The recipient of the money checked the total amount.
    As used in this sentence, the word *recipient* means MOST NEARLY

    A. receiver
    B. carrier
    C. borrower
    D. giver

16. Mr. Warren could not attend the luncheon because he had a prior appointment.
    As used in this sentence, the word *prior* means MOST NEARLY

    A. conflicting
    B. official
    C. previous
    D. important

17. The time allowed to complete the task was not adequate.
    As used in this sentence, the word *adequate* means MOST NEARLY

    A. long
    B. enough
    C. excessive
    D. required

18. The investigation unit began an extensive search for the information.
    As used in this sentence, the word *extensive* means MOST NEARLY

    A. complicated
    B. superficial
    C. thorough
    D. leisurely

19. The secretary answered the telephone in a courteous manner.
    As used in this sentence, the word *courteous* means MOST NEARLY

    A. businesslike
    B. friendly
    C. formal
    D. polite

20. Every good office worker needs basic skills.
    As used in this sentence, the word *basic* means MOST NEARLY

    A. fundamental
    B. advanced
    C. unusual
    D. outstanding

21. He turned out to be a good instructor.
    As used in this sentence, the word *instructor* means MOST NEARLY

    A. student
    B. worker
    C. typist
    D. teacher

22. The quantity of work in the office was under study.
    As used in this sentence, the word *quantity* means MOST NEARLY

    A. amount
    B. flow
    C. supervision
    D. type

23. The morning was spent examining the time records.
    As used in this sentence, the word *examining* means MOST NEARLY

    A. distributing
    B. collecting
    C. checking
    D. filing

24. The candidate filled in the proper spaces on the form.
    As used in this sentence, the word *proper* means MOST NEARLY

    A. blank
    B. appropriate
    C. many
    D. remaining

25. Employees who can produce a considerable amount of good work are very valuable.
    As used in this sentence, the word *considerable* means MOST NEARLY

    A. large
    B. potential
    C. necessary
    D. frequent

26. No person should assume that he knows more than anyone else.
    As used in this sentence, the word *assume* means MOST NEARLY

    A. verify
    B. hope
    C. suppose
    D. argue

27. The parties decided to negotiate through the night.
    As used in this sentence, the word *negotiate* means MOST NEARLY

    A. suffer
    B. play
    C. think
    D. bargain

28. Employees who have severe emotional problems may create problems at work.
    As used in this sentence, the word *severe* means MOST NEARLY

    A. serious
    B. surprising
    C. several
    D. common

29. Supervisors should try to be as objective as possible when dealing with subordinates.
    As used in this sentence, the word *objective* means MOST NEARLY

    A. pleasant   B. courteous   C. fair   D. strict

30. He advocated a new course of action.
    As used in this sentence, the word *advocated* means MOST NEARLY

    A. described   B. refused to discuss
    C. argued against   D. supported

31. A clerk who is assigned to make a *facsimile* of a report should make a copy which is

    A. exact   B. larger   C. smaller   D. edited

32. An employee must be a person of integrity.
    As used in this sentence, the word *integrity* means MOST NEARLY

    A. intelligence   B. competence
    C. honesty   D. keenness

33. A person who displays *apathy* is

    A. irritated   B. confused
    C. indifferent   D. insubordinate

34. The supervisor admonished the clerk for his tardiness.
    As used in this sentence, the word *admonished* means MOST NEARLY

    A. reproved   B. excused
    C. transferred   D. punished

35. A *lucrative* business is one which is

    A. unprofitable   B. gainful
    C. unlawful   D. speculative

36. To say that the work is *tedious* means MOST NEARLY that it is

    A. technical   B. interesting
    C. tiresome   D. confidential

37. A *vivacious* person is one who is

    A. kind   B. talkative
    C. lively   D. well-dressed

38. An *innocuous* statement is one which is

    A. forceful   B. harmless   C. offensive   D. brief

39. To say that the order was *rescinded* means MOST NEARLY that it was

    A. revised   B. canceled
    C. misinterpreted   D. confirmed

40. To say that the administrator *amplified* his remarks means MOST NEARLY that the remarks were

    A. shouted   B. expanded
    C. carefully analyzed D. summarized briefly

41. Peremptory commands will be resented in any office.
    As used in this sentence, the word *peremptory* means MOST NEARLY

    A. unexpected B. unreasonable
    C. military D. dictatorial

42. A clerk should know that the word *sporadic* means MOST NEARLY

    A. occurring regularly B. sudden
    C. scattered D. disturbing

43. To *vacillate* means MOST NEARLY to

    A. lubricate B. waver
    C. decide D. investigate

44. A *homogeneous* group of persons is characterized by its

    A. similarity B. teamwork
    C. discontent D. differences

45. A *vindictive* person is one who is

    A. prejudiced B. unpopular
    C. petty D. revengeful

Questions 46-48.

DIRECTIONS: Each of Questions 46 through 48 consists of a capitalized word followed by four suggested meanings of the word. Select the word or phrase which means MOST NEARLY the same as the capitalized word.

46. EQUILIBRIUM

    A. horse drawn B. unequal
    C. kind of library D. balance

47. RECIPROCATE

    A. to overcome B. to avenge
    C. to interchange D. to mix

48. REFRACTION

    A. increase B. refutation
    C. bending D. uniting

49. The surface of the metal was embossed.
    As used in this sentence, the word *embossed* means MOST NEARLY

    A. polished B. rough C. raised D. painted

50. Stoppage of water flow is often caused by dirt accumulating in an elbow.
    As used in this sentence, the word *accumulating* means MOST NEARLY

    A. clogging B. collecting
    C. rusting D. confined

KEY (CORRECT ANSWERS)

1. B	11. C	21. D	31. A	41. D
2. A	12. A	22. A	32. C	42. C
3. A	13. B	23. C	33. C	43. B
4. B	14. D	24. B	34. A	44. A
5. B	15. A	25. A	35. B	45. D
6. D	16. C	26. C	36. C	46. D
7. B	17. B	27. D	37. C	47. C
8. D	18. C	28. A	38. B	48. C
9. B	19. D	29. C	39. B	49. C
10. B	20. A	30. D	40. B	50. B

TEST 2

DIRECTIONS: Each question or incomplete statement is followed by several suggested answers or completions. Select the one that BEST answers the question or completes the statement. *PRINT THE LETTER OF THE CORRECT ANSWER IN THE SPACE AT THE RIGHT.*

1. Employees are responsible for the good care, proper maintenance and serviceable condition of property issued or assigned to their use.
   As used in the above sentence, the words *serviceable condition* means MOST NEARLY

   A. capable of being repaired
   B. fit for use
   C. ease of handling
   D. minimum cost

2. An employee shall be on the alert constantly for potential accident hazards.
   As used in the above sentence, the word *potential* means MOST NEARLY

   A. dangerous   B. careless   C. possible   D. frequent

3. The foreman is the keyman in safety in any working group.
   As used in the above sentence, the word *keyman* means MOST NEARLY

   A. watchman
   B. most important man
   C. man to whom to bring problems
   D. man who issues safety tools

4. It is best to find small defects before they can do great damage.
   As used in the above sentence, the word *defects* means MOST NEARLY

   A. faults   B. shorts   C. bearings   D. dangers

5. It is easier and cheaper to maintain equipment than to repair the equipment when it is too late.
   As used in the above sentence, the word *maintain* means MOST NEARLY

   A. buy good   B. use up
   C. keep in good condition D. throw away

6. Where the length of roadway pavement is less than 100 lineal feet, the requirement of cores may be waived. As used in the above sentence, the word *waived* means MOST NEARLY

   A. eliminated   B. enforced
   C. considered   D. postponed

7. Where only part of the sidewalk is to be relaid, the concrete shall match the predominant color of the existing sidewalk.
   As used in the above sentence, the word *predominant* means MOST NEARLY

   A. lightest   B. darkest
   C. main   D. contrasting

8. All stands must be substantially built so as not to create any hazard to passersby or other persons.
   As used in the above sentence, the word *hazard* means MOST NEARLY

   A. delay
   B. danger
   C. obstruction
   D. inconvenience

9. The lights shall be lighted and remain lighted every night during the hours prescribed.
   As used in the above sentence, the word *prescribed* means MOST NEARLY

   A. required
   B. not needed
   C. before midnight
   D. of darkness

10. The department in its discretion may direct that certain regulations be waived.
    As used in the above sentence, the word *discretion* means MOST NEARLY

    A. jurisdiction
    B. operation
    C. organization
    D. judgment

11. All canopy permits shall be posted in a conspicuous place at the entrance for which the permit is issued.
    As used in the above sentence, the word *conspicuous* means MOST NEARLY

    A. well known
    B. inaccessible
    C. easily observed
    D. obscure

12. Where a street opening is made by a licensed plumber, a plumber's bond may be filed in lieu of a street obstruction bond.
    As used in the above sentence, the words *in lieu of* means MOST NEARLY

    A. in addition to
    B. instead of
    C. immediately as
    D. appurtenant to

13. A solvent will also assist the paint in the penetration of porous surfaces.
    As used in the above sentence, the word *penetration* means MOST NEARLY

    A. covering
    B. protection
    C. cleaning
    D. entering

14. A painter should make sure he has sufficient paint to do the job.
    As used in the above sentence, the word *sufficient* means MOST NEARLY

    A. enough
    B. the right kind of
    C. the proper color of
    D. mixed

15. Religious bigotry is repugnant to all true democrats. As used in the above sentence, the word *repugnant* means MOST NEARLY

    A. dangerous
    B. distasteful
    C. revealing
    D. surprising

16. To obtain durability, exposed brickwork should be built of well-burned bricks.
    As used in the above sentence, the word *durability* means MOST NEARLY

    A. beauty
    B. water resistance
    C. strength
    D. long life

3 (#2)

Questions 17-19.

DIRECTIONS: Each of Questions 17 through 19 consists of a capitalized word followed by four suggested meanings of the word. Select the word or phrase which means MOST NEARLY the same as the capitalized word.

17. CONDUIT   17._____

    A. easy   B. behavior   C. channel   D. puzzle

18. CATALYSIS   18._____

    A. catacomb   B. charge
    C. fumigation   D. activation

19. INCREMENT   19._____

    A. accusation   B. expense
    C. addition   D. discrepancy

20. The machinist is machining a bearing housing of conventional design.   20._____
    As used in the above sentence, the word *conventional* means MOST NEARLY

    A. complicated   B. superior
    C. new   D. common

21. When turning a piece of tenacious metal on a lathe, a lubricant is used to prevent excessive friction by conducting the heat away.   21._____
    As used in the above sentence, the word *tenacious* means MOST NEARLY

    A. annealed   B. soft   C. tough   D. coarse

22. In a particular shop, a machinist is assigned to the task of coordinating various machining operations.   22._____
    As used in the above sentence, the word *coordinating* means MOST NEARLY

    A. repairing   B. replacing
    C. testing   D. scheduling

23. The employee made an insignificant error.   23._____
    As used in the above statement, the word *insignificant* means MOST NEARLY

    A. serious   B. accidental
    C. minor   D. hidden

24. Work areas must be kept clear of accumulations of equipment, materials, and rubbish.   24._____
    As used in the above sentence, the word *accumulations* means MOST NEARLY

    A. different kinds   B. piles
    C. interference   D. seldom used

25. All material in bags or bundles which are stored in tiers must be stacked and blocked so as to produce a stable pile.   25._____
    As used in the above sentence, the word *tiers* means MOST NEARLY

    A. groups   B. rooms   C. layers   D. sheds

26. Men must report all accidents, no matter how trivial. As used in the above sentence, the word *trivial* means MOST NEARLY

    A. often
    B. treated
    C. caused
    D. insignificant

27. The water level in the gage glass was dormant during the peak load conditions. As used in the above sentence, The word *dormant* means MOST NEARLY

    A. fluctuating
    B. inactive
    C. clean
    D. foaming

28. The instructor's words were understood but irrelevant. As used in the above sentence, the word *irrelevant* means MOST NEARLY

    A. unchallenging to the audience
    B. unconvincing to the audience
    C. not bearing upon the subject under discussion
    D. not based upon facts

29. An employee who is *zealous* in his work is one who is MOST NEARLY

    A. enthusiastic
    B. envious
    C. courteous
    D. patient

30. It is not the revolutions that destroy machinery, but the friction. As used in the above sentence, the word *friction* means MOST NEARLY

    A. rotation
    B. speed
    C. evolution
    D. resistance

31. A worker who makes a *significant* error makes one which is MOST NEARLY

    A. important
    B. accidental
    C. meaningless
    D. doubtful

32. A worker who is given *explicit* directions is given directions which are MOST NEARLY

    A. forceful
    B. erroneous
    C. confusing
    D. definite

33. If a supervisor gives *concise* instructions to his men daily, this means that his instructions are

    A. brief   B. wordy   C. changed   D. lengthy

34. If a foreman makes an *intricate* sketch of the bearing assembly, this means that the sketch is

    A. evident   B. obvious   C. clear   D. involved

35. *Gradual decrease in the width of an elongated object* is called a

    A. bevel   B. slope   C. spiral   D. taper

36. The worker showed great resentment towards his supervisor. As used in the above sentence, the word *resentment* means MOST NEARLY

    A. fear   B. dislike   C. affection   D. regard

37. Lubrication is an essential part of preventive maintenance.
    As used in the above sentence, the word *essential* means MOST NEARLY

    A. frequent   B. useful
    C. required   D. indispensable

38. Grader brakes are adequate for low speed working conditions.
    As used in the above sentence, the word *adequate* means MOST NEARLY

    A. good   B. strong   C. built   D. sufficient

39. The frame of a caterpillar grader consists of two cross braced members which converge to form a single arched beam.
    As used in the above sentence, the word *converge* means MOST NEARLY

    A. come together   B. are welded
    C. operate as a unit   D. are used

40. Mud is an impediment to work in many ways.
    As used in the above sentence, the word *impediment* means MOST NEARLY

    A. detriment   B. nuisance   C. hindrance   D. problem

41. *To make rows of small holes through a substance* defines the word

    A. penetrate   B. perforate   C. permeate   D. pulsate

42. A specification for electric work states: The Contractor, when performing work inside of the existing building, shall take all requisite measures to protect the furniture, shades, woodwork, plaster, and other items from any possible damage.
    As used in the above sentence, the word *requisite* means MOST NEARLY

    A. usual   B. requested   C. specified   D. necessary

43. When many statements in a worker's report are *redundant,* they are MOST NEARLY

    A. brief   B. wordy   C. adequate   D. regular

44. When an inspector's report is *concise,* it is MOST NEARLY

    A. rambling   B. unclear
    C. to the point   D. drawn out

45. An employee who is *dilatory* in his work is one who is MOST NEARLY

    A. expeditious   B. inconsistent
    C. inaccurate   D. slow

46. *To swing backward and forward* defines the word

    A. alternate   B. gesticulate
    C. oscillate   D. procrastinate

47. *A situation involving choices between equally unsatisfactory alternatives* is called a

    A. crisis   B. deadlock   C. dilemma   D. farce

48. A *statement of self-evident truth* is called a(n) 48.___

   A. adage
   B. axiom
   C. hypothesis
   D. theory

Questions 49-50.

DIRECTIONS: Questions 49 and 50 are to be answered on the basis of the following paragraph.

Extraneous noises developed by the system as installed in the building shall not be perceptible when the system is operating 6 db (sound volume) above the average operating level of the sound system.

49. The word *extraneous*, as used in the above paragraph, means MOST NEARLY 49.___

   A. meaningless
   B. foreign
   C. odd
   D. loud

50. The word *perceptible*, as used in the above paragraph, means MOST NEARLY 50.___

   A. receivable
   B. acceptable
   C. vibrating
   D. audible

KEY (CORRECT ANSWERS)

1. B	11. C	21. C	31. A	41. B
2. C	12. B	22. D	32. D	42. D
3. B	13. D	23. C	33. A	43. B
4. A	14. A	24. B	34. D	44. C
5. C	15. B	25. C	35. D	45. D
6. A	16. D	26. D	36. B	46. C
7. C	17. C	27. B	37. D	47. C
8. B	18. D	28. C	38. D	48. B
9. A	19. C	29. A	39. A	49. B
10. D	20. D	30. D	40. C	50. D

WORD MEANING

EXAMINATION SECTION
TEST 1

DIRECTIONS: Each question or incomplete statement is followed by several suggested answers or completions. Select the one that BEST answers the question or completes the statement. *PRINT THE LETTER OF THE CORRECT ANSWER IN THE SPACE AT THE RIGHT.*

1. Local responsibility for the relief of economic need long having been recognized as inadequate, the state and federal governments have established schemes of *categorical* assistance and social insurance.
   In the preceding sentence, the italicized word means MOST NEARLY

   A. conditional
   B. economic
   C. pecuniary
   D. classified

   1.____

2. When a person *vicariously* lives out his own problems in novels and plays, he is engaging in an experience that is, in terms of the italicized word in this sentence,

   A. dynamic
   B. monastic
   C. substituted
   D. dignified

   2.____

3. The Alcoholics Anonymous program, which in essence amounts to a *therapeutic* procedure, is codified into twelve steps. The italicized word in the preceding sentence means MOST NEARLY

   A. compensatory
   B. curative
   C. sequential
   D. volitional

   3.____

4. The professor developed a different central theme during every *semester*.
   The italicized word in the preceding sentence means MOST NEARLY

   A. bi-annual period of instruction
   B. orientation period
   C. slide demonstration
   D. weekly lecture series

   4.____

5. To say that the Community Chest movement seems to have been *indigenous* to the North American continent describes this movement, in terms of the italicized word in this sentence, MOST NEARLY as

   A. imported
   B. essential
   C. native
   D. homogeneous

   5.____

6. There should be no *opprobrium* attached to the term "second-hand housing" since every house is second-hand after the first occupancy.
   The italicized word in the preceding sentence means MOST NEARLY

   A. stigma   B. honor   C. rank   D. credit

   6.____

49

7. Clinics are now seeing many people who complain of seriously disturbed feelings and other symptoms relating to *traumatic* war experiences.
   In the preceding sentence, the italicized word means MOST NEARLY

   A. recent
   B. worldwide
   C. prodigious
   D. shocking

8. The nature of the *pathology* underlying the compulsion is obscure.
   In the preceding sentence, the italicized word means MOST NEARLY

   A. drive
   B. disease
   C. deterioration
   D. development

9. If the interests of a social welfare agency are concerned with bringing opportunities for self-help to underprivileged *ethnic* groups, its activities involve MOST NEARLY, in terms of the italicized word in this sentence,

   A. racial factors
   B. minority units
   C. religious affiliations
   D. economic conditions

10. Increased facilities for medical care (though interrupted to some extent by the *exigencies* of wartime) will safeguard the health of many children who in previous generations would have been doomed to an early death or to physical disability.
    In the preceding sentence, the MOST NEARLY CORRECT equivalent of the italicized word is

    A. obstacles
    B. occurrences
    C. extenuations
    D. exactions

11. He described a hypothetical situation to illustrate his point.
    In the preceding sentence, the word *hypothetical* means MOST NEARLY

    A. actual
    B. theoretical
    C. typical
    D. unusual

12. I gave tacit approval to my partner's proposed business changes.
    In the preceding sentence, the word *tacit* means MOST NEARLY

    A. enthusiastic
    B. partial
    C. silent
    D. written

13. Jones was considered an astute lawyer by the members of his profession.
    In the preceding sentence, the word *astute* means MOST NEARLY

    A. clever
    B. persevering
    C. poorly trained
    D. unethical

14. There were intimations even in early days of the way in which he would go.
    In the preceding sentence, the word *intimations* means MOST NEARLY

    A. hints
    B. patterns
    C. plans
    D. purposes

15. His last book was published posthumously.
    In the preceding sentence, the word *posthumously* means MOST NEARLY

    A. after the death of the author
    B. printed free by the publisher
    C. without a dedication
    D. without royalties

16. When he was challenged, he used every known subterfuge. In the preceding sentence, the word *subterfuge* means MOST NEARLY

    A. evasion to justify one's conduct
    B. means of attack to defend one's self
    C. medical device
    D. unconscious thought

17. His partner suggested a course of action that would alleviate the difficulties which confronted him.
    In the preceding sentence, the word *alleviate* means MOST NEARLY

    A. correct   B. lessen   C. remove   D. solve

18. Among the applicants for the new apartment, white collar workers were preponderant.
    In the preceding sentence, the word *preponderant* means MOST NEARLY

    A. considered not eligible   B. in evidence
    C. superior in number   D. the first to apply

19. The captain gave a lucid explanation of his plans for the coming campaign.
    In the preceding sentence, the word *lucid* means MOST NEARLY

    A. clear   B. graphic
    C. interesting   D. thorough

20. He led a sedentary life.
    In the preceding sentence, the word *sedentary* means MOST NEARLY

    A. aimless   B. exciting   C. full   D. inactive

21. His plan for the next campaign was very plausible.
    In the preceding sentence, the word *plausible* means MOST NEARLY

    A. appropriate   B. believable
    C. usable   D. valuable

22. The office manager thought it advisable to mollify his subordinate.
    The word *mollify*, as used in this sentence, means MOST NEARLY

    A. reprimand   B. caution   C. calm   D. question

23. The bureau chief adopted a dilatory policy.
    The word *dilatory*, as used in this sentence, means MOST NEARLY

    A. tending to cause delay
    B. acceptable to all affected
    C. severe but fair
    D. prepared with great care

24. He complained about the paucity of requests.
    The word *paucity*, as used in this sentence, means MOST NEARLY

    A. great variety   B. unreasonableness
    C. unexpected increase   D. scarcity

25. To say that an event is *imminent* means MOST NEARLY that it is

    A. near at hand
    B. unpredictable
    C. favorable or happy
    D. very significant

26. The general manager delivered a laudatory speech.
    The word *laudatory*, as used in this sentence, means MOST NEARLY

    A. clear and emphatic
    B. lengthy
    C. introductory
    D. expressing praise

27. We all knew of his aversion for performing statistical work.
    The word *aversion*, as used in this sentence, means MOST NEARLY

    A. training
    B. dislike
    C. incentive
    D. lack of preparation

28. The engineer was circumspect in making his recommendations.
    The word *circumspect*, as used in this sentence, means MOST NEARLY

    A. hostile   B. outspoken   C. biased   D. cautious

29. To say that certain clerical operations were *obviated* means MOST NEARLY that these operations were

    A. extremely distasteful
    B. easily understood
    C. made unnecessary
    D. very complicated

30. The interviewer was impressed with the client's demeanor. The word *demeanor*, as used in this sentence, means MOST NEARLY

    A. outward manner
    B. plan of action
    C. fluent speech
    D. extensive knowledge

31. To say that the information was *gratuitous* means MOST NEARLY that it was

    A. given freely
    B. deeply appreciated
    C. brief
    D. valuable

32. She considered the supervisor's action to be arbitrary. The word *arbitrary*, as used in this sentence, means MOST NEARLY

    A. inconsistent
    B. justifiable
    C. appeasing
    D. dictatorial

33. He sent the irate employee to the personnel manager. The word *irate* means MOST NEARLY

    A. irresponsible
    B. untidy
    C. insubordinate
    D. angry

34. An *ambiguous* statement is one which is

    A. forceful and convincing
    B. capable of being understood in more than one sense
    C. based upon good judgment and sound reasoning processes
    D. uninteresting and too lengthy

35. To *extol* means MOST NEARLY to

   A. summon   B. praise   C. reject   D. withdraw

36. The word *proximity* means MOST NEARLY

   A. similarity
   C. harmony
   B. exactness
   D. nearness

37. His friends had a detrimental influence on him.
    The word *detrimental* means MOST NEARLY

   A. favorable
   C. harmful
   B. lasting
   D. short-lived

38. The chief inspector relied upon the veracity of his inspectors.
    The word *veracity* means MOST NEARLY

   A. speed
   C. shrewdness
   B. assistance
   D. truthfulness

39. There was much diversity in the suggestions submitted.
    The word *diversity* means MOST NEARLY

   A. similarity
   C. triviality
   B. value
   D. variety

40. The survey was concerned with the problem of indigence.
    The word *indigence* means MOST NEARLY

   A. poverty
   C. intolerance
   B. corruption
   D. morale

41. The investigator considered this evidence to be extraneous.
    The word *extraneous* means MOST NEARLY

   A. significant
   C. not essential
   B. pertinent but unobtainable
   D. inadequate

42. He was surprised at the temerity of the new employee.
    The word *temerity* means MOST NEARLY

   A. shyness
   C. rashness
   B. enthusiasm
   D. self-control

43. The term *ex officio* means MOST NEARLY

   A. expelled from office
   B. a former holder of a high office
   C. without official approval
   D. by virtue of office or position

44. The aims of the students and the aims of the faculty often coincide.
    The word *coincide* means MOST NEARLY

   A. agree
   C. conflict
   B. are ignored
   D. are misinterpreted

45. The secretary of the department was responsible for setting up an index of relevant magazine articles.
    The word *relevant* means MOST NEARLY

    A. applicable
    B. controversial
    C. miscellaneous
    D. recent

46. One of the secretary's duties consisted of sorting and filing facsimiles of student term papers.
    The word *facsimiles* means MOST NEARLY

    A. bibliographical listings
    B. exact copies
    C. summaries
    D. supporting documentation

47. Stringent requirements for advanced physics courses often result in small class sizes.
    The word *stringent* means MOST NEARLY

    A. lengthy
    B. remarkable
    C. rigid
    D. vague

48. The professor explained that the report was too verbose to be submitted.
    The word *verbose* means MOST NEARLY

    A. brief
    B. specific
    C. general
    D. wordy

49. The faculty meeting pre-empted the conference room in the Dean's office.
    The word *pre-empted* means MOST NEARLY

    A. appropriated
    B. emptied
    C. filled
    D. reserved

50. The professor's credentials became a subject of controversy.
    The word *controversy* means MOST NEARLY

    A. annoyance
    B. debate
    C. envy
    D. review

KEY (CORRECT ANSWERS)

1. D	11. B	21. B	31. A	41. C
2. C	12. C	22. C	32. D	42. C
3. B	13. A	23. A	33. D	43. D
4. A	14. A	24. D	34. B	44. A
5. C	15. A	25. A	35. B	45. A
6. A	16. A	26. D	36. D	46. B
7. D	17. B	27. B	37. C	47. C
8. B	18. C	28. D	38. D	48. D
9. A	19. A	29. C	39. D	49. A
10. D	20. D	30. A	40. A	50. B

TEST 2

DIRECTIONS: Each question or incomplete statement is followed by several suggested answers or completions. Select the one that BEST answers the question or completes the statement. *PRINT THE LETTER OF THE CORRECT ANSWER IN THE SPACE AT THE RIGHT.*

1. The suspect was detained until a witness proved he could not have committed the crime. 1.____
   As used in this sentence, the word *detained* means MOST NEARLY

   A. suspected   B. accused   C. held   D. observed

2. The fireman's equilibrium improved shortly after he had stumbled out of the smoke-filled building. 2.____
   As used in this sentence, the word *equilibrium* means MOST NEARLY

   A. breathing   B. balance   C. vision   D. vigor

3. The water supply in the tank began to dwindle soon after the pumps were turned on. 3.____
   As used in this sentence, the word *dwindle* means MOST NEARLY

   A. grow smaller   B. whirl about
   C. become muddy   D. overflow

4. They thought his illness was feigned. 4.____
   As used in this sentence, the word *feigned* means MOST NEARLY

   A. hereditary   B. contagious
   C. pretended   D. incurable

5. The officer corroborated the information given by the fireman. 5.____
   As used in this sentence, the word *corroborated* means MOST NEARLY

   A. questioned   B. confirmed
   C. corrected   D. accepted

6. Only after an inspection were they even able to surmise what caused the fire. 6.____
   As used in this sentence, the word *surmise* means MOST NEARLY

   A. guess   B. discover   C. prove   D. isolate

7. Officers shall report all flagrant violations of regulations or laws by subordinates. 7.____
   As used in this sentence, the word *flagrant* means MOST NEARLY

   A. glaring   B. accidental
   C. habitual   D. minor

8. The man was cajoled into signing the contract. 8.____
   As used in this sentence, the word *cajoled* means MOST NEARLY

   A. bribed   B. coaxed   C. confused   D. forced

9. The announcement was met with general derision. 9.____
   As used in this sentence, the word *derision* means MOST NEARLY

   A. anger   B. applause   C. disbelief   D. ridicule

10. The speaker's words were moving but irrelevant.
    As used in this sentence, the word *irrelevant* means MOST NEARLY

    A. insincere
    B. not based upon facts
    C. not bearing upon the subject under discussion
    D. self-contradictory

11. The breakdown of the machine was due to a defective gasket.
    As used in this sentence, the word *gasket* means MOST NEARLY

    A. filter   B. piston
    C. sealer   D. transmission

12. The noise of the pneumatic drill disturbed the teacher.
    As used in this sentence, the word *pneumatic* means MOST NEARLY

    A. air pressure   B. electricity
    C. internal combustion   D. water pressure

13. He exercised the prerogatives of his office with moderation.
    As used in this sentence, the word *prerogatives* means MOST NEARLY

    A. burdens   B. duties
    C. opportunities D. privileges

14. He made his decisions after a cursory examination of the facts.
    As used in this sentence, the word *cursory* means MOST NEARLY

    A. biased   B. critical
    C. exhaustive D. hasty

15. John was appointed provisional chairman of the arrange-ments committee.
    As used in this sentence, the word *provisional* means MOST NEARLY

    A. official   B. permanent
    C. temporary   D. unofficial

16. After the bush is planted, the ground around it should be tamped.
    As used in this sentence, the word *tamped* means MOST NEARLY

    A. loosened   B. packed   C. raked   D. watered

17. The volcano was dormant during the time I visited the island.
    As used in this sentence, the word *dormant* means MOST NEARLY

    A. erupting   B. extinct
    C. inactive   D. threatening

18. A starter's gun is not considered to be a lethal weapon.
    As used in this sentence, the word *lethal* means MOST NEARLY

    A. criminal   B. deadly   C. offensive   D. reliable

19. At the crucial moment, the seismograph failed to function. As used in this sentence, the word *seismograph* means MOST NEARLY an instrument for measuring

    A. earthquakes   B. heartbeats
    C. humidity   D. nuclear radiation

20. The supervisor's instructions were terse.
    As used in this sentence, the word *terse* means MOST NEARLY

    A. detailed   B. harsh   C. vague   D. concise

21. He did not wish to evade these issues.
    As used in this sentence, the word *evade* means MOST NEARLY

    A. avoid   B. examine   C. settle   D. discuss

22. The prospects for an early settlement were dubious.
    As used in this sentence, the word *dubious* means MOST NEARLY

    A. strengthened   B. uncertain
    C. weakened   D. cheerful

23. The visitor was morose.
    As used in this sentence, the word *morose* means MOST NEARLY

    A. curious   B. gloomy   C. impatient   D. timid

24. He was unwilling to impede the work of his unit.
    As used in this sentence, the word *impede* means MOST NEARLY

    A. carry out   B. criticize   C. praise   D. hinder

25. The remuneration was unsatisfactory.
    As used in this sentence, the word *remuneration* means MOST NEARLY

    A. payment   B. summary
    C. explanation   D. estimate

26. A *recurring* problem is one that

    A. replaces a problem that existed previously
    B. is unexpected
    C. has long been overlooked
    D. comes up from time to time

27. His subordinates were aware of this magnanimous act. As used in this sentence, the word *magnanimous* means MOST NEARLY

    A. insolent   B. shrewd
    C. unselfish   D. threatening

28. The new employee is a zealous worker.
    As used in this sentence, the word *zealous* means MOST NEARLY

    A. awkward   B. untrustworthy
    C. enthusiastic   D. skillful

29. To *impair* means MOST NEARLY to

    A. weaken   B. conceal   C. improve   D. expose

30. The unit head was in a quandary.
    As used in this sentence, the word *quandary* means MOST NEARLY

    A. violent dispute   B. puzzling predicament
    C. angry mood   D. strong position

31. His actions were judicious.
    As used in this sentence, the word *judicious* means MOST NEARLY

    A. wise   B. biased   C. final   D. limited

32. His report contained many irrelevant statements.
    As used in this sentence, the word *irrelevant* means MOST NEARLY

    A. unproven   B. not pertinent
    C. hard to understand D. insincere

33. He was not present at the inception of the program.
    As used in this sentence, the word *inception* means MOST NEARLY

    A. beginning   B. discussion
    C. conclusion D. rejection

34. The word *solicitude* means MOST NEARLY

    A. request   B. isolation
    C. seriousness D. concern

35. He was asked to pacify the visitor.
    As used in this sentence, the word *pacify* means MOST NEARLY

    A. escort   B. interview   C. calm   D. detain

36. To say that a certain document is *authentic* means MOST NEARLY that it is

    A. fictitious B. well written
    C. priceless   D. genuine

37. A clerk who is *meticulous* in performing his work is one who is

    A. alert to improved techniques
    B. likely to be erratic and unpredictable
    C. excessively careful of small details
    D. slovenly and inaccurate

38. A pamphlet which is *replete* with charts and graphs is one which

    A. deals with the construction of charts and graphs
    B. is full of charts and graphs
    C. substitutes illustrations for tabulated data
    D. is in need of charts and graphs

39. His former secretary was diligent in carrying out her duties.
    The word *diligent* means MOST NEARLY

    A. incompetent B. cheerful
    C. careless   D. industrious

40. To *supersede* means MOST NEARLY to

    A. take the place of B. come before
    C. be in charge of   D. divide into equal parts

41. A person is a *tyro* if he is MOST NEARLY a

    A. charlatan   B. novice
    C. scholar   D. talebearer

42. A tenant who is *adamant* in his complaints about the noise emanating from the neighboring apartment is MOST NEARLY

    A. belligerent   B. justified
    C. petty   D. unyielding

43. The assistant, according to his supervisor's report, had performed his tasks assiduously. The word *assiduously* means MOST NEARLY

    A. diligently   B. expertly
    C. inefficiently   D. reluctantly

44. The current exigency of affairs at the Authority was given as the reason for the decision. The word *exigency* means MOST NEARLY

    A. conduct   B. investigation
    C. trend   D. urgency

45. The discovery of the defalcation was made by the manager. The word *defalcation* means MOST NEARLY

    A. damage   B. error   C. fraud   D. theft

46. The halcyon days that followed could not have been predicted. The word *halcyon* means MOST NEARLY

    A. eventful   B. festive
    C. frenzied   D. untroubled

47. The assistant submitted a sententious report after he had made his investigation. The word *sententious* means MOST NEARLY

    A. laudatory   B. pithy
    C. tentative   D. unfavorable

48. An assistant should be characterized as *saturnine* if he is MOST NEARLY

    A. apathetic   B. enigmatic   C. gloomy   D. sarcastic

49. A situation arising at a project is *anomalous* if the situation is MOST NEARLY

    A. irritating   B. perplexing
    C. recurrent   D. unusual

50. The Housing Authority did what it could to palliate the condition about which the tenants had complained.
The word *palliate* means MOST NEARLY

    A. reconsider   B. rectify
    C. relieve   D. remedy

KEY (CORRECT ANSWERS)

1. C	11. C	21. A	31. A	41. B
2. B	12. A	22. B	32. B	42. D
3. A	13. D	23. B	33. A	43. A
4. C	14. D	24. D	34. D	44. D
5. B	15. C	25. A	35. C	45. D
6. A	16. B	26. D	36. D	46. D
7. A	17. C	27. C	37. C	47. B
8. B	18. B	28. C	38. B	48. C
9. D	19. A	29. A	39. D	49. D
10. C	20. D	30. B	40. A	50. C

TEST 3

DIRECTIONS: Each question or incomplete statement is followed by several suggested answers or completions. Select the one that BEST answers the question or completes the statement. *PRINT THE LETTER OF THE CORRECT ANSWER IN THE SPACE AT THE RIGHT.*

1. The employees were skeptical about the usefulness of the new procedure. 1.____
   The word *skeptical*, as used in this sentence, means MOST NEARLY

   A. enthusiastic B. indifferent
   C. doubtful D. misinformed

2. He presented abstruse reasons in defense of his proposal. 2.____
   The word *abstruse*, as used in this sentence, means MOST NEARLY

   A. unnecessary under the circumstances
   B. apparently without merit or value
   C. hard to be understood
   D. obviously sound

3. A program of austerity is in effect in many countries. The word *austerity,* as used in this 3.____
   sentence, means MOST NEARLY

   A. rigorous self-restraint B. military censorship
   C. rugged individualism D. self-indulgence

4. The terms of the contract were abrogated at the last meeting of the board. 4.____
   The word *abrogated,* as used in this sentence, means MOST NEARLY

   A. discussed B. summarized
   C. agreed upon D. annulled

5. The enforcement of stringent regulations is a difficult task. 5.____
   The word *stringent,* as used in this sentence, means MOST NEARLY

   A. unreasonable B. strict
   C. unpopular D. obscure

6. You should not disparage the value of his suggestions. The word *disparage,* as used in 6.____
   this sentence, means MOST NEARLY

   A. ignore B. exaggerate
   C. belittle D. reveal

7. The employee's conduct was considered reprehensible by his superior. 7.____
   The word *reprehensible,* as used in this sentence, means MOST NEARLY

   A. worthy of reward or honor
   B. in accordance with rules and regulations
   C. detrimental to efficiency and morale
   D. deserving of censure or rebuke

8. He said he would emulate the persistence of his co-workers. The word *emulate,* as used 8.____
   in this sentence, means MOST NEARLY

   A. strive to equal B. acknowledge
   C. encourage D. attach no significance to

61

9. The revised regulations on discipline contained several mitigating provisions.
   The word *mitigating,* as used in this sentence, means MOST NEARLY

   A. making more effective
   B. containing contradictions
   C. rendering less harsh
   D. producing much criticism

10. The arrival of the inspector at the office on that day was fortuitous.
    The word *fortuitous,* as used in this sentence, means MOST NEARLY

    A. accidental
    B. unfortunate
    C. prearranged
    D. desirable

11. The development of the program received its real impetus in the recent action of the commissioner.
    The word *impetus,* as used in this sentence, means MOST NEARLY

    A. formulation
    B. impediment
    C. implementation
    D. stimulus

12. However, the purpose is not to be pedantic but to be practical.
    The word *pedantic,* as used in this sentence, means MOST NEARLY

    A. affected
    B. philosophical
    C. progressive
    D. scientific

13. There is much just criticism of the dilatoriness with which many large organizations perform their work and the red tape that is required in the discharge of official duties.
    The word *dilatoriness,* as used in this sentence, means MOST NEARLY

    A. complications
    B. delay
    C. dilations
    D. splendor

14. If it appears that this report moves occasionally into the general field of administrative problems, your indulgence is asked, since it seems to us that voices should be heard wherever possible in behalf of sound, scientific public administration.
    The word *indulgence,* as used in this sentence, means MOST NEARLY

    A. criticism
    B. assistance
    C. forbearance
    D. concentration

15. The supervisor's chief functions as leader are to develop the individuals under him and to integrate them into a cooperative team.
    The word *integrate,* as used in this sentence, means MOST NEARLY

    A. develop   B. mold   C. unify   D. work

16. The impression is widespread that it is inherently impossible to secure the same efficiency and economy in the administration of public affairs that can be secured in the conduct of private undertakings.
    The word *inherently,* as used in this sentence, means MOST NEARLY

    A. admittedly
    B. internally
    C. naturally
    D. practically

17. The production manager had followed an opportunistic policy and had met new requirements as they appeared.
    The word *opportunistic,* as used in this sentence, means MOST NEARLY

    A. efficient
    B. expedient
    C. farsighted
    D. important

18. Therein is epitomized the agricultural revolution which, hand in hand with the industrial revolution, is rebuilding the country and our social life.
    The word *epitomized,* as used in this sentence, means MOST NEARLY

    A. annotated
    B. described
    C. expatriated
    D. summarized

19. A periodic appraisal of the method of effectuating decisions is important.
    The word *effectuating,* as used in this sentence, means MOST NEARLY

    A. affecting
    B. developing
    C. fulfilling
    D. making

20. The classifications of filing material in this office are, then, artificial and overlapping, and are designed for transient convenience.
    The word *transient,* as used in this sentence, means MOST NEARLY

    A. basic
    B. local
    C. operating
    D. temporary

21. From a research standpoint, there is hardly a paucity of material for us to consider.
    The word *paucity,* as used in this sentence, means MOST NEARLY

    A. abundance
    B. adequate amount
    C. insufficiency
    D. unsatisfactory quality

22. This assignment was handled expeditiously.
    The word *expeditiously* means MOST NEARLY

    A. clumsily
    B. without preparation
    C. speedily
    D. on a trial basis

23. Miss Lind is scrupulous in performing her duties.
    The word *scrupulous* means MOST NEARLY

    A. slow
    B. conscientious
    C. careless
    D. gracious

24. To *apprise* means MOST NEARLY to

    A. award
    B. inform
    C. dispossess
    D. discover

25. His report on this matter is opportune.
    The word *opportune* means MOST NEARLY

    A. timely
    B. biased
    C. hostile
    D. hopeful

26. His actions had a deleterious effect on the other employees.
    The word *deleterious* means MOST NEARLY

    A. restraining   B. highly pleasing
    C. harmful   D. misleading

27. The size of the staff was increased, and the gain in output was commensurate.
    The word *commensurate* means MOST NEARLY

    A. praiseworthy   B. enormous
    C. of equal extent   D. trivial in proportion

28. Miss Hunter is assiduous in keeping these records.
    The word *assiduous* means MOST NEARLY

    A. negligent   B. untrained
    C. unrestricted   D. diligent

29. His bookkeeper said that our account was dormant.
    The word *dormant* means MOST NEARLY

    A. inadequate   B. transferred
    C. inactive   D. overdrawn

30. The supervisor's criticisms were caustic.
    The word *caustic* means MOST NEARLY

    A. sarcastic and severe   B. unfair and undeserved
    C. ominous but justified   D. fitful and unsteady

31. The word *impediment* means MOST NEARLY

    A. hindrance   B. trick or deception
    C. insinuation   D. urgent matter

32. This procedure did not preclude errors in judgment.
    The word *preclude* means MOST NEARLY

    A. arise from   B. prevent
    C. account for   D. define

33. The statements made at the initial conference were retracted at a subsequent meeting.
    The word *retracted* means MOST NEARLY

    A. developed   B. criticized
    C. endorsed   D. withdrawn

34. He was unwilling to supplant his immediate superior.
    The word *supplant* means MOST NEARLY

    A. fill the needs of   B. request aid from
    C. take the place of   D. withhold support for

35. Miss Olin has a prepossessing manner.
    The word *prepossessing* means MOST NEARLY

    A. authoritative   B. likable
    C. apologetic   D. deceiving

36. The methods used to solve these critical problems were analogous.
    The word *analogous* means MOST NEARLY

    A. similar
    B. unconventional
    C. clever
    D. unsound

37. This letter appears to have been written by some indigent person.
    The word *indigent,* as used in this sentence, means MOST NEARLY

    A. foreign-born
    B. needy
    C. uneducated
    D. angry

38. The conference began under auspicious circumstances.
    The word *auspicious,* as used in this sentence, means MOST NEARLY

    A. favorable
    B. chaotic
    C. questionable
    D. threatening

39. An inordinate amount of work was assigned to the newly appointed clerk.
    The word *inordinate,* as used in this sentence, means MOST NEARLY

    A. unanticipated
    B. adequate
    C. inexcusable
    D. excessive

40. The report which was obtained surreptitiously was very detailed and fully documented.
    The word *surreptitiously,* as used in this sentence, means MOST NEARLY

    A. stealthily
    B. a short time ago
    C. with great difficulty
    D. unexpectedly

41. We all knew him to be a man of probity.
    The word *probity,* as used in this sentence, means MOST NEARLY

    A. culture
    B. proven ability
    C. integrity
    D. dignity and poise

42. He made a cursory study of the problem before starting on the assignment.
    The word *cursory,* as used in this sentence, means MOST NEARLY

    A. detailed
    B. secret
    C. hasty
    D. methodical

43. The regulation had a salutary effect upon the members of the staff.
    The word *salutary,* as used in this sentence, means MOST NEARLY

    A. disturbing
    B. beneficial
    C. confusing
    D. premature

44. The solicitous supervisor discussed the employee's grievances with them.
    The word *solicitous,* as used in this sentence, means MOST NEARLY

    A. concerned
    B. impartial
    C. wise
    D. experienced

45. The employee categorically denied all responsibility for the error.
    The word *categorically,* as used in this sentence, means MOST NEARLY

    A. repeatedly
    B. loudly
    C. hesitantly
    D. absolutely

46. No stipend was specified in the agreement. 46._____
    The word *stipend,* as used in this sentence, means MOST NEARLY

    A. statement of working conditions
    B. receipt for payment
    C. compensation for services
    D. delivery date

47. The supervisor pointed out that the focus of the study was not clear. 47._____
    The word *focus,* as used in this sentence, means MOST NEARLY

    A. end   B. objective   C. follow-up   D. location

48. The faculty of the department agreed that the departmental program was deficient. 48._____
    The word *deficient,* as used in this sentence, means MOST NEARLY

    A. excellent   B. inadequate
    C. demanding   D. sufficient

49. The secretary was asked to type a rough draft of a college course syllabus. 49._____
    The word *syllabus,* as used in this sentence, means MOST NEARLY

    A. directory of departments and services
    B. examination schedule
    C. outline of a course of study
    D. rules and regulations

50. The college offered a variety of seminars to upperclassmen. 50._____
    The word *seminars,* as used in this sentence, means MOST NEARLY

    A. reading courses with no formal supervision
    B. study courses for small groups of students engaged in research under a teacher
    C. guidance conferences with grade advisors
    D. work experiences in different occupational fields

KEY (CORRECT ANSWERS)

1. C	11. D	21. C	31. A	41. C
2. C	12. A	22. C	32. B	42. C
3. A	13. B	23. B	33. D	43. B
4. D	14. C	24. B	34. C	44. A
5. B	15. C	25. A	35. B	45. D
6. C	16. C	26. C	36. A	46. C
7. D	17. B	27. C	37. B	47. B
8. A	18. D	28. D	38. A	48. B
9. C	19. C	29. C	39. D	49. C
10. A	20. D	30. A	40. A	50. B

WORD MEANING
EXAMINATION SECTION
TEST 1

DIRECTIONS: For the following questions, select the word or group of words lettered A, B, C, D, or E that means MOST NEARLY the same as the word in capital letters. *PRINT THE LETTER OF THE CORRECT ANSWER IN THE SPACE AT THE RIGHT.*

1. The lane was NARROW and led to a mountain lake.   1._____
   - A. attractive
   - B. not wide
   - C. overgrown
   - D. rough
   - E. without trees

2. Blow the horn as you APPROACH the gate.   2._____
   - A. discover
   - B. leave
   - C. draw near
   - D. pass through
   - E. unlock

3. It was part of our BARGAIN that you should wash dishes.   3._____
   - A. agreement   B. debt   C. goal   D. plan   E. wish

4. I shall remember that little valley FOREVER.   4._____
   - A. often   B. yet   C. always   D. next   E. no more

5. The boy was EAGER to go on the trip.   5._____
   - A. able   B. afraid   C. anxious   D. likely   E. willing

6. The children were having a DISPUTE over the boy.   6._____
   - A. conversation
   - B. crying spell
   - C. disagreement
   - D. performance
   - E. tantrum

7. The man was punished for his BRUTAL act.   7._____
   - A. bloody
   - B. cruel
   - C. deadly
   - D. defenseless
   - E. ugly

8. We LAUNCHED our new business with great hope for the future.   8._____
   - A. concluded   B. started   C. pursued   D. steered   E. watched

9. The two streets INTERSECT at the edge of town.   9._____
   - A. run parallel
   - B. change names
   - C. end
   - D. become thoroughfares
   - E. cross

10. She suffered from an UNCOMMON disease.   10._____
    - A. ordinary   B. painful   C. contagious   D. rare   E. new

67

11. The antique chair was very FRAGILE.

    A. delicate   B. worn   C. beautiful   D. well-made   E. useless

12. They picked EDIBLE mushrooms.

    A. poisonous   B. well-formed   C. unusual   D. large   E. eatable

13. He found the reception at the airport very GRATIFYING.

    A. surprising   B. deafening   C. pleasant
    D. disagreeable   E. impolite

14. DEFECTIVE brakes caused the mishap.

    A. old-fashioned   B. uneven   C. squeaking
    D. unused   E. faulty

15. After a little EXERTION the box was moved.

    A. argument   B. delay   C. coaxing   D. effort   E. planning

KEY (CORRECT ANSWERS)

1. B   6. C
2. C   7. B
3. A   8. B
4. C   9. E
5. C   10. D

11. A
12. E
13. C
14. E
15. D

TEST 2

DIRECTIONS: For the following questions, select the word or group of words lettered A, B, C, D, or E that means MOST NEARLY the same as the word in capital letters. *PRINT THE LETTER OF THE CORRECT ANSWER IN THE SPACE AT THE RIGHT.*

1. The RAPIDITY of the attack surprised us. 1.____
   - A. power
   - B. effectiveness
   - C. possibility
   - D. strangeness
   - E. swiftness

2. She enjoyed CONVERSING with her friends. 2.____
   - A. meeting B. laughing C. talking D. dining E. traveling

3. There was a small VENT near the end of the tube. 3.____
   - A. cap B. screw C. opening D. joint E. pump

4. With great CAUTION we opened the barn door. 4.____
   - A. care B. fear C. distrust D. danger E. difficulty

5. The old man's coat was THREADBARE. 5.____
   - A. spotted B. tight C. new D. ill-made E. shabby

6. I was sorry that I could not decide OTHERWISE. 6.____
   - A. immediately
   - B. differently
   - C. favorably
   - D. positively
   - E. eagerly

7. The GIGANTIC switchboard controlled all the lights in the theatre. 7.____
   - A. complicated
   - B. up-to-date
   - C. automatic
   - D. huge
   - E. stationary

8. The balls were made of SYNTHETIC rubber. 8.____
   - A. artificial B. hard C. cheap D. imported E. crude

9. He was MERELY a servant in the house. 9.____
   - A. occasionally
   - B. in no way
   - C. unhappily
   - D. formerly
   - E. no more than

10. The prisoner CONFERRED with his lawyer. 10.____
    - A. argued
    - B. interfered
    - C. dined
    - D. sympathized
    - E. consulted

11. The soldier's GALLANTRY went unnoticed. 11.____
    - A. strength
    - B. fright
    - C. disobedience
    - D. injury
    - E. bravery

12. The music was chosen for its SOOTHING effect.

    A. tuneful   B. calming   C. magic   D. exciting   E. solemn

13. The owners were advised to REINFORCE the wall.

    A. rebuild   B. lengthen   C. lower   D. strengthen   E. repaint

14. They performed their duties with UTMOST ease.

    A. noticeable   B. some   C. surprising   D. greatest   E. increasing

15. We picnicked near a CASCADE.

    A. pond   B. camp   C. waterfall   D. trail   E. slope

KEY (CORRECT ANSWERS)

1. E
2. C
3. C
4. A
5. E
6. B
7. D
8. A
9. E
10. E
11. E
12. B
13. D
14. D
15. C

TEST 3

DIRECTIONS: For the following questions, select the word or group of words lettered A, B, C, D, or E that means MOST NEARLY the same as the word in capital letters. *PRINT THE LETTER OF THE CORRECT ANSWER IN THE SPACE AT THE RIGHT.*

1. The chairman was anxious to ADJOURN the meeting.
   A. conduct   B. attend   C. start   D. address   E. close

2. The gown was made of a GLOSSY fabric.
   A. shiny   B. embroidered   C. many-colored
   D. transparent   E. expensive

3. An ocean voyage in a small boat can be very HAZARDOUS.
   A. thrilling   B. slow   C. dangerous   D. rough   E. tiresome

4. The weatherman predicted VARIABLE winds.
   A. drying   B. strong   C. cool   D. light   E. changeable

5. Not long after the play began, the children began to FIDGET.
   A. clap   B. move restlessly
   C. cry   D. laugh aloud
   E. shriek

6. That person has a habit of MEDDLING.
   A. stumbling   B. interfering   C. play jokes
   D. cheating   E. being late

7. Young children are frequently INQUISITIVE.
   A. curious   B. saucy   C. restless   D. shy   E. tearful

8. The FALSITY of the report was apparent at first glance.
   A. uselessness   B. untidiness   C. incompleteness
   D. incorrectness   E. disagreeableness

9. Orders were given to LIBERATE the prisoners by noon.
   A. question   B. transfer   C. free   D. sentence   E. fingerprint

10. She is HABITUALLY late for her dental appointments.
    A. usually   B. seldom   C. extremely   D. slightly   E. never

11. The soldiers were given SPACIOUS living quarters.
    A. pleasant   B. well-aired   C. crowded
    D. well-furnished   E. roomy

12. The witnesses gave STRAIGHTFORWARD answers.

    A. hasty   B. frank   C. conflicting   D. helpful   E. serious

13. His income EXCEEDS that of his brother.

    A. is less regular than
    B. is greater than
    C. is the same as
    D. is less than
    E. is spent sooner than

14. He SHUNNED all of his neighbors.

    A. disapproved   B. welcomed   C. quarreled with
    D. avoided   E. insulted

15. Many of the natives are ILLITERATE.

    A. unable to read   B. unclean   C. unable to vote
    D. unmanageable   E. sickly

KEY (CORRECT ANSWERS)

1. E
2. A
3. C
4. E
5. B
6. B
7. A
8. D
9. C
10. A
11. E
12. B
13. B
14. D
15. A

TEST 4

DIRECTIONS: For the following questions, select the word or group of words lettered A, B, C, D, or E that means MOST NEARLY the same as the word in capital letters. *PRINT THE LETTER OF THE CORRECT ANSWER IN THE SPACE AT THE RIGHT.*

1. We have always found this medicine to be RELIABLE.   1._____
   - A. dependable
   - B. easy to use
   - C. pleasant-tasting
   - D. bitter
   - E. fast-acting

2. The cloth was left to BLEACH in the sun.   2._____
   - A. dry   B. soak   C. whiten   D. shrink   E. rot

3. The work is ORDINARILY done on time.   3._____
   - A. seldom
   - B. without fail
   - C. necessarily
   - D. hardly ever
   - E. usually

4. Jim is a very DISCOURTEOUS boy.   4._____
   - A. impolite   B. daring   C. untruthful   D. uneasy   E. cautious

5. Paris is noted for its BOULEVARDS.   5._____
   - A. crooked streets
   - B. parks
   - C. art galleries
   - D. churches
   - E. broad avenues

6. The group formed the SEMICIRCLE quickly.   6._____
   - A. half-circle
   - B. double circle
   - C. complete circle
   - D. uneven
   - E. very small circle

7. The machine that he designed was PORTABLE.   7._____
   - A. business-like
   - B. practical
   - C. of foreign manufacture
   - D. easily transported
   - E. difficult to use

8. The food supply DWINDLED during the winter.   8._____
   - A. spoiled
   - B. became less
   - C. froze
   - D. was wasted
   - E. was rationed

9. The vase was one of the PERMANENT exhibits at the museum.   9._____
   - A. historical
   - B. lasting
   - C. popular
   - D. artistic
   - E. well-planned

10. We could not understand why he left so ABRUPTLY.   10._____
    - A. suddenly
    - B. soon
    - C. absent-mindedly
    - D. mysteriously
    - E. noisily

KEY (CORRECT ANSWERS)

1. A
2. C
3. E
4. A
5. E
6. A
7. D
8. B
9. B
10. A

WORD MEANING
EXAMINATION SECTION
TEST 1

DIRECTIONS: For the following questions, select the word or group of words lettered A, B, C, D, or E that means MOST NEARLY the same as the word in capital letters. *PRINT THE LETTER OF THE CORRECT ANSWER IN THE SPACE AT THE RIGHT.*

1. The directors plan to EXPAND the factory. 1.____
   A. shut down B. remodel C. enlarge D. erect E. occupy

2. The CAPTIVE pleaded for mercy. 2.____
   A. savage B. spy C. jailer D. officer E. prisoner

3. The policeman CONSOLED the weeping child. 3.____
   A. found B. carried home C. scolded
   D. comforted E. played with

4. On these slopes there is very little VEGETATION. 4.____
   A. traffic B. rocky soil C. plant life
   D. moisture E. bird life

5. The pupil was criticized for his SLIPSHOD work. 5.____
   A. slow B. childish C. uncompleted
   D. careless E. incorrect

6. The names of characters in plays are usually FICTITIOUS. 6.____
   A. odd B. imaginary C. pleasant-sounding
   D. easy to remember E. well-known

7. The most interesting part of the book was the PREFACE. 7.____
   A. title page B. introduction C. table of contents
   D. cover design E. illustrations

8. The bullet PENETRATED the wall. 8.____
   A. entered into B. dented C. bounded off
   D. passed over E. weakened

9. The large mustache made the actor look VILLAINOUS. 9.____
   A. dignified B. slightly older C. very wicked
   D. untidy E. uncomfortable

10. They hoped to EXTERMINATE the insects. 10.____
    A. destroy B. collect C. classify
    D. experiment with E. drive away

75

11. It is my CONVICTION that you are wrong. 11.___
    A. fear   B. fault   C. firm belief   D. imagination   E. recollection

12. A good employee is always PUNCTUAL. 12.___
    A. polite   B. neat   C. thoughtful   D. prompt   E. truthful

13. The actor played a JUVENILE role. 13.___
    A. lovesick   B. humorous   C. criminal   D. modern   E. youthful

14. In business letters we state our business CONCISELY. 14.___
    A. accurately   B. fully   C. briefly   D. politely   E. officially

15. We found that the goods on sale were of INFERIOR quality. 15.___
    A. second-rate   B. excellent   C. lasting
    D. noticeable   E. surprising

KEY (CORRECT ANSWERS)

1. C   6. B
2. E   7. B
3. D   8. A
4. C   9. C
5. D   10. A

11. C
12. D
13. E
14. C
15. A

TEST 2

DIRECTIONS: For the following questions, select the word or group of words lettered A, B, C, D, or E that means MOST NEARLY the same as the word in capital letters. *PRINT THE LETTER OF THE CORRECT ANSWER IN THE SPACE AT THE RIGHT.*

1. The sword has a KEEN edge.

   A. bright   B. sharp   C. steel   D. polished   E. rough

2. He STARTLED the boy who was trying to unlock the car.

   A. surprised   B. punished   C. chased   D. arrested   E. helped

3. FORTHCOMING events were listed on the club bulletin board.

   A. weekly   B. interesting   C. outstanding
   D. social   E. approaching

4. The lawyer's next question ASTOUNDED the witness.

   A. misled   B. amazed   C. depressed   D. pleased   E. angered

5. In his hand the hiker was carrying a large STAFF.

   A. pack   B. loaf   C. stick
   D. musical instrument E. garment

6. We nervously awaited the doctor's VERDICT.

   A. arrival   B. call   C. approval
   D. decision   E. prescription

7. The hikers noticed several CREVICES in the rocks.

   A. plants   B. uneven spots   C. fossils
   D. water holes   E. cracks

8. Such training helps to make a boy SELF-SUFFICIENT.

   A. clever   B. healthy   C. conceited
   D. independent   E. uncomfortable

9. The door was left AJAR.

   A. slightly opened   B. unhinged   C. unguarded
   D. unlocked   E. completely blocked

10. They talked about INSIGNIFICANT matters.

    A. unimportant   B. thrilling   C. puzzling
    D. unpleasant   E. secret

77

11. The child was given a good mark for DEPORTMENT.

    A. intelligence B. attendance C. health D. behavior E. neatness

12. Because of PRIOR engagements, she refused the invitation.

    A. personal   B. more urgent   C. more attractive
    D. future   E. earlier

13. The delegates will CONVENE at noon.

    A. dine B. vote C. debate D. assemble E. agree

14. Modern methods bring more REVENUE to the farmer.

    A. taxes B. income C. produce D. leisure E. acreage

15. The machine has MANUAL controls.

    A. self-acting   B. double   C. hand-operated
    D. simple   E. handmade

KEY (CORRECT ANSWERS)

1. B
2. A
3. E
4. B
5. C

6. D
7. E
8. D
9. A
10. A

11. D
12. E
13. D
14. B
15. C

TEST 3

DIRECTIONS: For the following questions, select the word or group of words lettered A, B, C, D, or E that means MOST NEARLY the same as the word in capital letters. *PRINT THE LETTER OF THE CORRECT ANSWER IN THE SPACE AT THE RIGHT.*

1. Grandfather ACQUIRED ten acres of pasture land.

   A. obtained B. plowed C. sold D. leased E. desired

2. A feeling of EXHAUSTION came over the players during the game.

   A. fear B. extreme tiredness C. overconfidence
   D. unsteadiness E. complete happiness

3. We pitied the child in the GRIMY clothes.

   A. ill-fitting B. secondhand C. poorly made
   D. dirty E. ragged

4. The mechanic's calculations were APPROXIMATE.

   A. nearly exact B. remarkable C. hastily made
   D. worthless E. mathematically correct

5. A COMPETENT young woman was given the position.

   A. busy B. pretty C. capable
   D. friendly E. good-natured

6. We had BARELY finished by six o'clock.

   A. easily B. only just C. partly
   D. more or less E. unexpectedly

7. His second offense was more GRIEVOUS than his first. GRIEVOUS means *most nearly*

   A. serious B. stupid C. deliberate D. excusable E. peculiar

8. All air traffic was SUSPENDED during the emergency.

   A. turned back B. speeded up C. stopped
   D. relieved E. repaired

9. The antics of the monkeys DIVERTED the children.

   A. upset B. amused C. surprised D. disgusted E. frightened

10. The man SURVIVED his three sisters.

    A. loved B. envied C. outlived D. destroyed E. excelled

11. Franklin was a man of EXCEPTIONAL ability.

    A. well-trained   B. active   C. mechanical
    D. self-educated   E. unusual

12. Their aim seems to be to THWART our plans.

    A. simplify   B. direct   C. rely on
    D. block   E. keep up with

13. He heard the warning cry of another PEDESTRIAN.

    A. agent   B. walker   C. passenger
    D. workingman   E. traffic officer

14. They boasted about the SUPERIORITY of their product.

    A. beauty   B. abundance   C. excellence
    D. popularity   E. permanence

15. We considered their point of view ABSURD.

    A. disgusting   B. old-fashioned   C. insincere
    D. reasonable   E. foolish

KEY (CORRECT ANSWERS)

1. A
2. B
3. D
4. A
5. C

6. B
7. A
8. C
9. B
10. C

11. E
12. D
13. B
14. C
15. E

TEST 4

DIRECTIONS: For the following questions, select the word or group of words lettered A, B, C, D, or E that means MOST NEARLY the same as the word in capital letters. *PRINT THE LETTER OF THE CORRECT ANSWER IN THE SPACE AT THE RIGHT.*

1. Our neighbor PURCHASED his home last year.
   A. bought   B. rented   C. painted   D. remodeled   E. built

2. The only sound was the STEADY ticking of the clock.
   A. noisy   B. rapid   C. regular   D. cheerful   E. tiresome

3. The desks in our room are STATIONARY.
   A. heavy   B. not movable   C. metal
   D. easily adjustable   E. standard

4. Before signing the papers, Mr. Edmond consulted his ATTORNEY.
   A. banker   B. clerk   C. lawyer   D. secretary   E. employer

5. We IMITATE those whom we admire.
   A. protect   B. attract   C. study   D. copy   E. appreciate

6. They reached the SUMMIT of the mountain by noon.
   A. base   B. wooded area   C. side
   D. face   E. top

7. The motorist HEEDED the signals.
   A. worried about   B. passed by   C. took notice of
   D. laughed at   E. disagreed with

8. The SEVERITY of their criticism upset us.
   A. purpose   B. harshness   C. method
   D. suddenness   E. unfairness

9. We made a very LEISURELY trip to California.
   A. roundabout   B. unhurried   C. unforgettable
   D. tiresome   E. speedy

10. The little girl shook her head VIGOROUSLY.
    A. sadly   B. hopefully   C. sleepily
    D. thoughtfully   E. energetically

KEYS (CORRECT ANSWERS)

1. A
2. C
3. B
4. C
5. D

6. E
7. C
8. B
9. B
10. E

WORD MEANING
EXAMINATION SECTION
TEST 1

DIRECTIONS: For the following questions, select the word or group of words lettered A, B, C, D, or E that means MOST NEARLY the same as the word in capital letters. *PRINT THE LETTER OF THE CORRECT ANSWER IN THE SPACE AT THE RIGHT.*

1. The CONFLAGRATION spread throughout the entire city.

    A. hostilities   B. confusion   C. rumor   D. epidemic   E. fire

2. The firemen PURGED the gas tank after emptying its contents.

    A. sealed   B. punctured   C. exposed   D. cleansed   E. buried

3. Rules must be applied with DISCRETION.

    A. impartiality   B. judgment   C. severity
    D. patience   E. consistency

4. The officer and his men ASCENDED the stairs as rapidly as they could.

    A. went up   B. washed down   C. chopped
    D. shored up   E. inspected

5. The store's refusal to accept delivery of the merchandise was a violation of the EXPRESS provisions of the contract.

    A. clear   B. implied
    C. penalty   D. disputed
    E. complicated

6. Mr. Walsh could not attend the luncheon because he had a PRIOR appointment.

    A. conflicting   B. official   C. previous
    D. important   E. subsequent

7. The time allowed to complete the task was not ADEQUATE.

    A. long   B. enough   C. excessive   D. required   E. stated

8. The investigation unit began an EXTENSIVE search for the information.

    A. complicated   B. superficial   C. thorough
    D. leisurely   E. cursory

9. The secretary answered the telephone in a COURTEOUS manner.

    A. businesslike   B. friendly
    C. formal   D. gruff
    E. polite

10. The RECIPIENT of the money checked the total amount.

    A. receiver   B. carrier   C. borrower   D. giver   E. sender

11. The College offered a variety of SEMINARS to upperclassmen.

    A. reading courses with no formal supervision
    B. study courses for small groups of students engaged in research under a teacher
    C. guidance conferences with grade advisors
    D. work experience in different occupational fields
    E. luncheon discussions

12. The Dean pointed out that the FOCUS of the study was not clear.

    A. end   B. objective   C. follow-up   D. location   E. basis

13. The faculty of the Anthropology Department agreed that the departmental program was DEFICIENT.

    A. excellent   B. inadequate   C. demanding   D. sufficient   E. dilatory

14. The secretary was asked to type a rough draft of a course SYLLABUS.

    A. directory of departments and services   B. examination schedule
    C. outline of a course of study   D. rules and regulations
    E. schedule of meetings

15. There is an item in a painting contract relating to INSOLVENCY.

    A. the improper mixing of paint
    B. the use of improper materials
    C. taking excessive time to complete the contract
    D. bankruptcy
    E. the use of water

KEY (CORRECT ANSWERS)

1. E	6. C	11. B
2. D	7. B	12. B
3. B	8. C	13. B
4. A	9. E	14. C
5. A	10. A	15. D

TEST 2

DIRECTIONS: For the following questions, select the word or group of words lettered A, B, C, D, or E that means MOST NEARLY the same as the word in capital letters. *PRINT THE LETTER OF THE CORRECT ANSWER IN THE SPACE AT THE RIGHT.*

1. The number of applicants exceeded the ANTICIPATED figure.   1.____

   A. expected   B. required   C. revised   D. necessary   E. hoped-for

2. The clerk was told to COLLATE the pages of the report.   2.____

   A. destroy   B. edit   C. correct   D. assemble   E. fasten

3. Mr. Jones is not AUTHORIZED to release the information.   3.____

   A. inclined   B. pleased   C. permitted   D. trained   E. expected

4. The secretary chose an APPROPRIATE office for the meeting.   4.____

   A. empty
   B. decorated
   C. nearby
   D. suitable
   E. inexpensive

5. The employee performs a COMPLEX set of tasks each day.   5.____

   A. difficult   B. important   C. pleasant   D. large   E. secret

6. The foreman INVESTIGATED the sewer to see whether it was clogged.   6.____

   A. compelled   B. diverted   C. opened   D. improved   E. examined

7. The foreman SUPERVISED the work closely.   7.____

   A. criticized
   B. neglected
   C. praised
   D. superintended
   E. reviewed

8. ILLICIT connections are often found during sewer inspections.   8.____

   A. damaged   B. legal   C. poor   D. unlawful   E. clogged

9. The sewage in the manhole was floating SLUGGISHLY.   9.____

   A. buoyantly   B. odiferously   C. slowly   D. swiftly   E. evenly

10. It is most COMMON to find sewer pipes made of either clay or concrete.   10.____

    A. characteristic
    B. inordinate
    C. prevalent
    D. retiring
    E. vulgar

11. He needed public assistance because he was INCAPACITATED.   11.____

    A. uneducated
    B. unreliable
    C. uncooperative
    D. discharged
    E. disabled

12. The caseworker explained to the client that signing the document was COMPULSORY.   12.___

    A. temporary   B. required
    C. different   D. comprehensive
    E. usual

13. The woman's actions did not JEOPARDIZE her eligibility for benefits.   13.___

    A. delay   B. reinforce   C. determine   D. endanger   E. enhance

14. The material is PUTRESCIBLE.   14.___

    A. compacted   B. liable to burn   C. heavy
    D. liable to rot   E. liable to clog

15. Older incinerator plants are handstoked and fed INTERMITTENTLY.   15.___

    A. constantly   B. heavily   C. periodically
    D. with a shovel   E. every few minutes

KEY (CORRECT ANSWERS)

1. A	6. E	11. E
2. D	7. D	12. B
3. C	8. D	13. D
4. D	9. C	14. D
5. A	10. C	15. C

TEST 3

DIRECTIONS: For the following questions, select the word or group of words lettered A, B, C, D, or E that means MOST NEARLY the same as the word in capital letters. *PRINT THE LETTER OF THE CORRECT ANSWER IN THE SPACE AT THE RIGHT.*

1. The foreman made an ABSURD remark. 1._____

   A. misleading   B. ridiculous   C. unfair   D. wicked   E. artful

2. The electrician was ADEPT at his job. 2._____

   A. co-operative   B. developed
   C. diligent   D. skilled
   E. inept

3. The foreman stated that the condition was GENERAL. 3._____

   A. artificial   B. prevalent   C. timely   D. transient   E. likely

4. The asphalt worker engages in a HAZARDOUS job. 4._____

   A. absorbing   B. dangerous   C. demanding
   D. difficult   E. uninteresting

5. The foreman made a TRIVIAL mistake. 5._____

   A. accidental   B. dangerous
   C. obvious   D. serious
   E. unimportant

6. No DEVIATION from the specifications will be allowed unless the same has been previously authorized by the engineer. 6._____

   A. violation   B. variation   C. complete change
   D. authorized change   E. inference

7. The contractor shall SAFEGUARD all points, stakes, grade marks, monuments, and bench marks, made or established on or near the line of the work. 7._____

   A. watch closely   B. guard against theft
   C. prevent damage to   D. replace
   E. control

8. Bitumen-sand bed shall consist of sand with cut-back asphalt COMBINED in definite proportions by weight. 8._____

   A. together   B. mixed   C. added   D. placed   E. undiluted

9. The material was quite DESICCATED. 9._____

   A. hard   B. dangerous   C. soft   D. spongy   E. dry

10. Malice was PATENT in all of his remarks. 10._____

    A. elevated   B. evident   C. threatening   D. foreign   E. implicit

87

11. A Chaplain shall have the COMPARABLE rank of Inspector.

    A. false   B. superior   C. equal   D. presumed   E. ordinary

12. Pushcarts and DERELICT automobiles shall be delivered to the bureau of incumbrances.

    A. dilapidated   B. abandoned   C. delinquent
    D. contraband   E. unusable

13. When the EXIGENCIES of the service shall so require, a captain may assign a patrolman from the outgoing platoon to house duty.

    A. needs   B. conveniences
    C. changes   D. increases
    E. exits

14. There is a provision for the award of a medal for merit for an act of outstanding bravery, performed in the line of duty, at IMMINENT personal hazard of life.

    A. impending   B. inherent   C. certain   D. great   E. eminent

15. A member of the department shall not communicate with a railroad company for the purpose of EXPEDITING the issue of a transportation pass,

    A. extorting   B. procuring   C. demanding
    D. hastening   E. extending

KEY (CORRECT ANSWERS)

1. B	6. B	11. C
2. D	7. C	12. B
3. B	8. B	13. A
4. B	9. E	14. A
5. E	10. B	15. D

TEST 4

DIRECTIONS: For the following questions, select the word or group of words lettered A, B, C, D, or E that means MOST NEARLY the same as the word in capital letters. *PRINT THE LETTER OF THE CORRECT ANSWER IN THE SPACE AT THE RIGHT.*

1. The EXTANT copies of the document were found in the safe.   1.____

   A. existing   B. original   C. forged   D. duplicate   E. torn

2. The recruit was more COMPLAISANT after the captain spoke to him.   2.____

   A. calm   B. affable   C. irritable   D. confident   E. arrogant

3. The man was captured under highly CREDITABLE circumstances.   3.____

   A. doubtful   B. believable   C. praiseworthy
   D. unexpected   E. unbelievable

4. The new employee appeared DIFFIDENT.   4.____

   A. contrary   B. haughty   C. conceited   D. unsure   E. confident

5. His superior officers were more SAGACIOUS than he.   5.____

   A. upset   B. obtuse   C. absurd   D. verbose   E. shrewd

KEY (CORRECT ANSWERS)

1. A
2. B
3. C
4. D
5. E

www.ingramcontent.com/pod-product-compliance
Lightning Source LLC
Chambersburg PA
CBHW082127230426
43671CB00015B/2829